To Sophie

Thank you so much!
I hope you enjoy the book.

[signature]

x

HOLLIE WOOD

DINNER
at Hol's

QUICK & EASY RECIPES FOR DELICIOUS FAMILY DINNERS

Introduction

Our family of four – myself, my husband Steve and our two children Harry and Lottie – have always been a foodie family and love to cook together, trying new things in the kitchen. My little ones love to help me out with my creations and are more inclined to try new foods and flavours when they have helped to create it themselves. Steve, whom I've been married to for ten years now, wasn't really into cooking before this journey started, but now cooks lots of lovely meals, often following my recipes from Instagram! I have always had a love for cooking, following on from my mum, who was always in the kitchen cooking or baking. She even let me cook our Thursday night dinners from the age of 11! Since I was young, I've loved to try flavour combinations from all over the world and the recipes in this book take inspiration from Indian, Chinese, and American cuisines.

The aim of this book is to share quick and easy meals that are simple to make, yet full of flavour and delicious to eat. I know the struggle of having to cook for a family of four when you're lacking ideas about what to make, but hopefully this book will provide inspiration for those of you needing a little extra creative help in the kitchen. The tips I've added at the end of each recipe also give you different options for adapting the meal, substituting different ingredients, and altering intense flavours and spices to suit everyone's tastes. I know that my family and I love extra spice, but others not so much, so these tips allow you to adapt recipes to different preferences and enjoy stress-free, comfortable cooking for everyone. Additionally, all the meals included in this book are calorie counted, allowing you to enjoy the foods you love while eating in moderation. I believe that we shouldn't restrict what we eat in order to be healthy, but we can find the perfect balance between eating what we love in satisfying, super tasty meals while maintaining a balanced diet.

Before we get into the delicious recipes, I'd like to say a few thank yous. Thank you to my husband, Steve, for being the most supportive and helpful partner I could wish to be by my side on this incredible journey. Thank you to my readers, for buying this book and trying these fantastic recipes. I hope you enjoy making them as much as I enjoyed creating them. Finally, thank you to my followers, who have supported me on this amazing culinary journey. I couldn't quite believe it when I started receiving messages from people who have tried and loved my recipes – it is the best feeling in the world! People getting in touch to tell me how my recipes have helped them to fall in love with cooking again makes all the hard work worth it. This book is dedicated to the people who support me day in and day out on social media: recreating my recipes, sending me photos of your creations, and showing me immeasurable love and kindness along the way. Thank you!

About the Author

Hollie is the creator of Dinner At Hol's, a family-friendly Instagram account and cookbook designed to inspire readers to try creative, affordable and balanced recipes at home. As a skilled culinary expert with over 15 years of experience, Hollie loves to create family-friendly recipes that are both affordable and easy to make. Her recipe content is not only mouth-watering, but it also encourages home cooks to think outside the box and be daring with their food choices. Hollie's expertise provides the guidance to whip up quick and tasty meals that will have the whole family craving more.

Starting her Instagram profile during lockdown, Hollie wanted to journal her cooking journey at home, sharing her love of food with others and documenting all her meals in one place. The main aim of the Instagram page was to share creative recipes that are easy and quick to make for dinner, while being calorie-conscious and part of a balanced diet. As her Instagram following grew, more and more people joined Hollie's foodie community, asking for culinary advice and sharing their own food creations based on the recipes.

Since going full-time on her foodie venture in 2022, Hollie's presence on social media has blown up, with a following of over 200k across Instagram and TikTok who love her quick and easy dinner ideas. Since gaining popularity, her cooking creations have led to multiple brand deals, including the home appliance brands Instant and Progress Cookshop, and a collaboration with one of Hollie's all-time favourite ingredients, Boursin, which is featured in several recipes in this book.

In addition to her impressive cooking skills, Hollie is also a natural teacher and guide in the kitchen. She provides beautiful insight into her culinary techniques and inspires her followers to get creative and try new things, often with the help of her children and husband, keeping the recipes easy yet adventurous. Whether you're an experienced home cook or just starting out, Hollie's recipes are sure to help you up your game and expand your culinary horizons.

Contents

FAMILY FAVOURITES

20 MINUTE AND UNDER MEALS

ONE POT WONDERS

COMFORT MEALS

SIDES AND SMALL BITES

Calorie Counting

Calorie counting is an important part of my culinary experience, and I incorporate it into all my recipes. For me, tracking calories helps to maintain a balanced diet when it comes to eating delicious foods. I believe that we can absolutely eat the foods that we love, simply in moderation. That is why I've included calorie counts for all the recipes in this book, helping you to keep track of your calorie intake while still making mouth-watering meals.

I've calculated the calories in my recipes based on the exact ingredients I used; however, do take into account that other brands of those products will differ slightly, so the total calorie count may vary. I've also included any optional ingredients within the calorie count, so that anything added to the dish is already accounted for; that way you don't have to worry about calculating extras.

To track my own calories per meal, I like to use a calorie counting app called Nutracheck. This app requires a small monthly subscription fee, but in my opinion it's worth the money and is a lot more user-friendly than most of the free apps that are available. So, you might benefit from the app too as it's very easy to use; simply add the ingredients into the app for every meal and that's it!

Instant Vortex Plus

Ready

Air Fry   Roast   Bake   Reheat   Grill   Dehydrate

Temp/   Time   Light

Key Ingredient Swaps

Single cream can be swapped out for a dairy-free cream. Alternatively, you could use cream cheese, crème fraiche or natural yoghurt. However, remember that when making these swaps, the total calorie count of the meal can change.

In place of chicken, why not try a meat-free alternative such as Quorn, halloumi, paneer, or tofu? This creates tasty dishes for the vegetarians out there, or if you just fancy a meat-free meal for dinner.

Instead of minced beef or pork, you could use a meat-free substitute such as lentils, Quorn, mushrooms, or beans. All of these are tasty options, and a great source of fibre.

Instead of the cornflake coating used for meat in some of my recipes, try breadcrumbs or panko breadcrumbs. Alternatively, you can use a crispy rice cereal or even crushed crisps to get that delicious crunch.

For all my pasta and spaghetti dishes, feel free to change the pasta shape to any you prefer. Just take into consideration that different types of pasta can have different cooking times, so read the cooking instructions on the packet carefully.

In place of cheese, why not try a low-fat cheese alternative? Or swap it for dairy-free cheese.

If you don't have any fresh garlic to hand and your recipe calls for it, don't worry – just use garlic purée instead! Remember, 1 teaspoon of garlic purée is equivalent to 1 clove of fresh garlic.

If you don't have any fresh peppers or onions in your fridge, you can always swap these for frozen and pre-sliced if you prefer. The benefits of using frozen veggies are that they're often cheaper, last longer than fresh ones, and are still healthy and nutritious.

FAMILY FAVOURITES

CALORIES
567
PER PORTION

Sweet chilli and halloumi definitely have a special place in my heart; I think it's the salty cheese with that sweet but spicy sauce that just takes this burger to the next level.

Crispy Chicken and Sweet Chilli Halloumi Burger

Servings: 4 | Prep time: 10 minutes | Cooking time: 20 minutes

100g cornflakes, crushed
1 tbsp smoked paprika
1 tbsp garlic granules
½ tbsp oregano
1 tsp salt
4 chicken breasts, butterflied
2 eggs or egg whites, whisked
Cooking oil spray
140g halloumi, sliced
5 tbsp sweet chilli sauce
4 tbsp lighter mayonnaise
4 burger buns
Rocket (optional)

Preheat the oven to 220°c/200°c fan or an air fryer to 180°c.

Start by adding all the seasonings to the crushed cornflakes. Dip the chicken breasts into the whisked egg and then into the seasoned cornflakes so they are fully coated.

Spray the coated chicken with oil and pop in the air fryer or oven for around 20 minutes.

Meanwhile, fry off the halloumi in a pan with 1 tablespoon of the sweet chilli sauce until browned and sticky.

Mix the remaining sweet chilli and mayonnaise together. Toast the buns cut side down in a dry pan.

Once the chicken is cooked, assemble the burgers with a crispy chicken breast and slices of sweet chilli halloumi inside each bun, topped with a handful of rocket if you like. Serve and enjoy.

Tips: For vegetarian burgers, you could swap to a meat-free alternative instead of the chicken or coat some more halloumi in the cornflakes.

I love a pasta salad and this one must be my all-time favourite. It's perfect as a main dish and you can also serve it as a side at a barbecue or picnic.

Chicken Shawarma Pasta Salad

Servings: 4 | Prep time: 5 minutes | Cooking time: 35 minutes

For the shawarma

500g skinless and boneless chicken thighs

2 tsp garlic purée

2 tsp ginger purée

1 tsp ground cumin

1 tsp ground turmeric

1 tsp ground coriander

1 tsp paprika

½ tsp ground cinnamon

½ tsp chilli flakes (optional)

For the pasta salad

300g short pasta

½ cucumber, diced

2 red peppers, diced

1 red onion, finely diced

For the garlic sauce

4 tbsp fat-free natural yoghurt

4 tbsp mayonnaise

½ lemon, juiced

2 cloves of garlic, minced

Salt, to taste

Preheat the oven to 220°c/200°c fan or an air fryer to 180°c.

Put all the ingredients for the shawarma into a large bowl and mix well to coat the chicken thighs, then transfer to a roasting tin or the air fryer.

Cook the chicken in the oven or air fryer for about 30-35 minutes or until cooked through.

Meanwhile, boil your pasta in salted water until cooked and then rinse it under the cold tap to cool. Drain well and set aside.

Once the chicken is cooked, slice it up and set aside, allowing it to cool a little.

For the garlic sauce, mix all the ingredients together in a bowl and then season to taste.

In a large serving bowl, combine the cooled pasta with the sliced chicken and garlic sauce, then add the cucumber, peppers and onion.

Give your salad a good mix, then serve and enjoy.

This moreish pasta salad is bound to become one of your favourites. The spiced chicken, creamy sauce and crisp veggies will leave you wanting more of this tasty dish.

Chicken Tikka Pasta Salad

Servings: 4 | Prep time: 5 minutes | Cooking time: 35 minutes

For the chicken tikka

500g skinless and boneless chicken thighs

200g natural fat-free yoghurt

½ lemon, juiced

2 tsp garlic purée

2 tsp ginger purée

2 tsp ground coriander

1 tsp each of ground cumin, ground turmeric, paprika, garam masala and salt

½ tsp ground cinnamon

½ tsp chilli powder (optional)

For the pasta salad

300g short pasta

½ cucumber, diced

2 red peppers, diced

1 red onion, finely diced

For the tikka sauce

4 tbsp fat-free natural yoghurt

4 tbsp mayonnaise

½ lemon, juiced

2 cloves of garlic, minced

1 tbsp mango chutney (optional)

1 tbsp mild curry paste

Salt, to taste

Preheat the oven to 220°c/200°c fan or an air fryer to 180°c.

Put all the ingredients for the chicken tikka into a large bowl and mix well to coat the chicken thighs, then transfer to a roasting tin or the air fryer.

Cook the chicken in the oven or air fryer for about 30-35 minutes or until cooked through.

Meanwhile, boil your pasta in salted water until cooked and then rinse it under the cold tap to cool. Drain well and set aside.

Once the chicken is cooked, slice it up and set aside, allowing it to cool a little.

For the tikka sauce, mix all the ingredients together in a bowl and then season to taste.

In a large serving bowl, combine the cooled pasta with the sliced chicken and tikka sauce, then add the cucumber, peppers and onion.

Give your salad a good mix, then serve and enjoy.

My mum and stepdad used to make these chicken skewers every time we went on holiday in the caravan. They are perfect for the barbecue and amazing with a salad or in a pitta. So simple yet so full of flavour!

Lemon, Garlic and Ginger Chicken Skewers

Servings: 4 | Prep time: 5 minutes + 30 minutes marinating | Cooking time: 10 minutes

500g chicken breast, diced

1 tbsp paprika

1 tsp chilli flakes, or to taste

4 tsp garlic purée

2 tsp ginger purée

½ lemon, juiced

1 tbsp oil

1 tsp salt

Mix all the ingredients together in a large bowl and leave to marinate for 30 minutes. If you have time, leave overnight.

Preheat the oven to 220°c/200°c fan or an air fryer to 180°c.

Thread the marinated chicken onto the skewers.

Cook for around 10-15 minutes in the oven or air fryer until cooked through.

Serve and enjoy.

Tips: If you are using wooden skewers, make sure to soak them in water first to prevent them from burning. For me, metal skewers work best as they help to cook the chicken from the inside.

If you follow me on social media then you know how much I love a one pot rice dish, and this is no exception. Cooking all the ingredients in just one dish makes this an easy yet delicious recipe.

One Pot Pizza Rice

Servings: 4 | Prep time: 5 minutes | Cooking time: 20 minutes

20 slices of pepperoni

1 onion, diced

2 peppers, diced

2 cloves of garlic, grated

4 tbsp tomato purée

1 tbsp white wine vinegar

1 tbsp oregano

1 tsp salt

250g basmati rice

600ml chicken stock

80g grated mozzarella

Cut half the pepperoni slices into quarters and leave the other half whole. In a large frying pan with a lid, fry the quartered pepperoni.

Once the oils have released and the pepperoni is starting to go crispy, add the onion and peppers.

When they have softened, add the garlic and cook for another few minutes.

Stir in the tomato purée and cook for a minute before adding the white wine vinegar.

Allow that to cook out and then add the oregano, salt and uncooked basmati rice. Give it a good mix and then pour in the stock.

Turn the heat right down low and place the lid on. Cook for about 10-15 minutes or until all the stock has been absorbed and the rice is fully cooked, adding more liquid if necessary.

Place in an ovenproof dish, top with the mozzarella and the whole pepperoni slices, then place under the grill until golden and bubbling. Serve and enjoy.

Tips: You can add any toppings you like to this dish and even make it vegetarian by taking out the pepperoni and adding more veggies like mushrooms and sweetcorn, or a meat-free alternative.

It was my little boy, Harry, that came up with the idea for this recipe. It has all the flavours of a classic hotdog but in a cheesy, comforting pasta dish.

One Pot Hotdog Macaroni Cheese

Servings: 4 | Prep time: 5 minutes | Cooking time: 20 minutes

1 tbsp light butter

3 onions, thinly sliced

4 hotdogs, sliced

2 tbsp ketchup

2 tbsp American mustard

300g macaroni

500ml chicken stock

500ml milk, warmed

120g grated cheese (I use a mix of cheddar and mozzarella)

1 tsp mustard (optional)

Salt and pepper

Fresh parsley, to garnish

For the onion breadcrumbs

2 slices of bread

1 tbsp onion granules

½ tsp salt

1 tbsp light butter

Start by melting the butter in a large pan and frying the onions until they're soft and caramelised. Add the sliced hotdogs to fry for a few minutes.

Stir the ketchup and mustard into the onions and hotdogs, then take a spoonful of this mixture out and set aside for later.

Add the uncooked pasta to the pan along with the stock and milk. Let this simmer for about 15-20 minutes until the pasta is fully cooked, gradually adding more liquid if needed.

Meanwhile, prepare the breadcrumb topping. Blitz the bread in a food processor to make fine crumbs, then stir in the onion granules and salt.

In a clean frying pan, melt the butter and then fry the onion breadcrumbs until crispy and golden. Pour into a bowl and set aside.

Add half the cheese to the pan of pasta and stir until melted, then stir in the mustard if using. Season with salt and pepper to taste.

Transfer the pasta into an ovenproof dish, then sprinkle the remaining cheese on top.

Place the dish under a hot grill until golden and bubbling, then top with the reserved hotdog mix, crispy onion breadcrumbs and fresh parsley.

Add an extra drizzle of ketchup and mustard if you like, then serve and enjoy.

Smoky BBQ sauce, crispy bacon, juicy chicken, and melty, gooey cheese: what more could you want from a burger? These easy burgers are perfect for a midweek treat or a tasty 'fakeaway' when you want something that takes little effort but has maximum flavour.

Easy Hunter's Chicken Burgers

Servings: 4 | Prep time: 5 minutes | Cooking time: 25 minutes

4 skinless and boneless chicken thighs

1 tbsp smoked paprika

½ tbsp garlic granules

½ tbsp oregano

1 tsp salt

4 rashers of bacon

4 tbsp BBQ sauce

60g cheddar cheese, grated

4 brioche burger buns

Preheat the oven to 220°c/200°c fan or an air fryer to 190°c.

On a flat surface, bash your chicken thighs with a rolling pin until they are thinner and even in size.

Season the chicken with the smoked paprika, garlic granules, oregano and salt.

Lay the bacon on top of the flattened chicken thighs, then put them in the oven or air fryer for 15 minutes.

Spread the BBQ sauce and cheese on top of the bacon wrapped chicken, then cook for another 10 minutes or until the chicken is cooked through.

Meanwhile, toast the brioche burger buns cut sides down in a dry frying pan to crisp them up.

Assemble the burgers with a cheesy chicken thigh inside each brioche bun. Serve and enjoy.

Tips: You can always swap the thighs for chicken breasts if you prefer. Just make sure to reduce the cooking time slightly so the meat doesn't dry out and stays moist and tender.

This roasted red pepper pasta is something that should always be on the menu, no matter what the occasion. It's amazing hot or cold, perfect for packed lunches, and goes down a treat as a barbecue side.

Creamy Roasted Red Pepper Pasta

Servings: 4 | Prep time: 5 minutes | Cooking time: 30 minutes

4 red peppers, sliced

2 red onions, sliced

4 cloves of garlic, finely grated

1 tsp thyme

1 tbsp oil

300g pasta

120ml light single cream

25g parmesan, grated (optional)

Preheat the oven to 220°c/200°c fan or an air fryer to 180°c.

Put the peppers, onions, garlic, and thyme on a baking tray. Drizzle with the oil and mix well so the vegetables are all coated, then cook in the oven or air fryer for 20-30 minutes.

Meanwhile, place the pasta into a pan of boiling water with plenty of salt to cook until al dente.

Once the peppers are soft and a little blackened, take the baking tray out of the oven. Pop the roasted vegetables into a blender and blend.

Put the blended red pepper sauce into a pan on a low heat and stir in the cream.

Season to taste with salt and then add the cooked and drained pasta to the sauce.

Splash in a little pasta water and stir until you get a nice silky sauce.

Sprinkle over the parmesan if using. Serve and enjoy.

Tips: You can add any kind of protein you like to this dish. Chicken, bacon or chorizo would work really well.

What's not to love about this dinner? Although it's obviously not a traditional lasagne, it has all the elements that make an incredibly tasty dish. We absolutely love it.

Lasagne-Style Orzo

Servings: 4 | Prep time: 5 minutes | Cooking time: 30-40 minutes

500g lean beef mince

150g smoked bacon, diced

1 onion, finely diced

2 medium carrots, finely diced

3 peppers, finely diced

2 cloves of garlic, minced

1 tbsp tomato purée

1 tbsp Italian mixed herbs

Salt and pepper, to taste

500g passata

300g orzo

1 litre hot chicken stock

120g cheddar, finely grated

Fresh basil or parsley, to garnish

For the béchamel

2 tbsp light butter

2 tbsp plain flour

300ml milk, warmed

1 tsp mustard (optional)

Salt and pepper, to taste

Start by browning the mince and bacon in a large pan. Once browned, add the onion, carrots, and peppers. Once the vegetables have softened, add the garlic and cook for another minute.

Stir in the tomato purée and herbs, cook for a minute, then season to taste and add the passata. Allow this sauce to cook for at least 20 minutes but if you have time, cook for an hour on a low heat.

Meanwhile, make your béchamel. Melt the butter in a saucepan, then add the flour and mix to form a roux. Let this cook for a few minutes, stirring often to make sure it doesn't catch.

Slowly start adding the warmed milk to the roux, bit by bit, stirring continuously until you get a thick sauce. Stir in the mustard and season to taste, then set the béchamel aside for now.

Going back to your tomato sauce, stir in the orzo and then add the stock bit by bit until the orzo is cooked. You may not need the full litre of stock. Keep stirring so nothing sticks to the bottom.

Once the orzo is cooked and the stock has been incorporated, level the surface and then spoon the béchamel on top. Spread it out to cover the orzo mix and then sprinkle with the grated cheddar.

Pop the dish under a hot grill until golden and bubbling, then garnish with the fresh basil or parsley. Serve and enjoy.

These bacon and cheese smash burgers really are a thing of beauty. Oozy, gooey cheese, crispy bacon and caramelised onions all brought together with a juicy burger and a sweet brioche bun. Complete heaven.

Bacon and Cheese Smash Burger

Servings: 4 | Prep time: 2 minutes | Cooking time: 20 minutes

2 large onions

1 tbsp oil

1 tsp salt

4 rashers of bacon

500g lean beef mince

Salt and pepper

4 light cheese slices

4 brioche burger buns

4 tbsp ketchup

4 tbsp mustard

Salad of your choice
(I use lettuce and gherkins)

Finely slice the onions while you warm up a frying pan on a medium heat. Fry the onions gently in the oil until soft and caramelised, seasoning with the salt.

Once cooked, take the onions out and cook the bacon in the same pan until crispy.

Once the bacon is done to your liking, take that out the pan and place to the side for later.

Divide the beef mince into 4 equal balls, place them into the frying pan and smash them down so that they're nice and flat, then season generously with salt and pepper.

Cook the burger patties for 4 minutes and then flip over. Place a cheese slice and a rasher of bacon on top of each burger and cook for another 4 minutes.

Meanwhile, toast the brioche buns and then add the ketchup and mustard to both the top and the bottom halves.

Add your salad to the bottom half of each bun and then place the burgers on top, followed by the caramelised onions and then the top half of the bun. Serve and enjoy.

Tips: You can swap out the ketchup and mustard for any sauce that you fancy. A burger sauce works very well or even a garlic mayo; it's up to you.

CALORIES 644 PER PORTION

This was one of the first recipes I created that went big on social media and I can see why! We all love hunter's chicken; it's a tried and tested flavour combination. But pop it together in a one pot rice dish and you've got a winner!

One Pot Hunter's Chicken Rice

Servings: 4 | Prep time: 5 minutes | Cooking time: 20 minutes

500g chicken, diced

150g bacon, diced

1 tbsp BBQ seasoning

1 tbsp smoked paprika

1 onion, finely diced

2 cloves of garlic, finely grated

1 tbsp tomato purée

2 tbsp BBQ sauce

250g basmati rice

600ml chicken stock

120g grated cheese (I use a mix of cheddar, Red Leicester and mozzarella)

Extra BBQ sauce and fresh parsley, to garnish

Fry the chicken, bacon, BBQ seasoning, and paprika in a large frying pan until brown.

Add the onions and cook until soft, then stir in the garlic, tomato purée and BBQ sauce.

Cook for a few minutes before adding the uncooked basmati rice and the chicken stock.

Place a lid on the pan and cook on a low heat for about 20 minutes or until the rice is fully cooked, adding more liquid if needed.

Make sure you don't stir the rice after it's cooked. Instead, fluff it with a fork to separate the grains and then transfer the mixture to an ovenproof dish.

Sprinkle with the cheese and then place under the grill until golden and bubbling.

Drizzle over the extra BBQ sauce and top with parsley to taste, then serve and enjoy.

Tips: I would suggest using a smoky BBQ sauce rather than a sweet one here, as it just seems to work so much better.

CALORIES
343
PER
PORTION

These tasty bites really don't need much of an introduction! It's hard to find anything not to love about these little bites of heaven. Juicy, well-seasoned chicken, crispy coating, and a super garlicky butter to drizzle over means flavour perfection!

Crispy Chicken Kiev Bites

Servings: 4 | Prep time: 4 minutes | Cooking time: 15 minutes

500g chicken breasts, diced
1 tbsp garlic granules
1 tbsp mixed herbs
1 tsp salt
2 eggs or egg whites, whisked
100g cornflakes, crushed
4 tbsp light butter
3 cloves of garlic, finely grated
1 tbsp chopped fresh parsley

Preheat the oven to 220°c/200°c fan or an air fryer to 180°c.

In a large bowl, season the chicken with the garlic granules, mixed herbs, and salt.

In two more separate bowls, coat the chicken in the whisked egg and then cover with the crushed cornflakes.

Place the chicken bites in the oven or air fryer for 10-15 minutes (depending on how big they are).

Meanwhile, melt the butter in a small bowl and then add the garlic, parsley, and salt to taste. Stir well until the ingredients are combined.

Toss the hot crispy chicken bites in the garlic butter until coated.

Serve and enjoy.

Tips: These chicken bites are also amazing with a teaspoon of chilli flakes added to the garlic butter for a little bit of a kick.

This dinner is based on a recipe that my mum used to make for me when I was younger. I love the combination of tarragon with pork mince and find that it works so well with the cheesy topping.

Cheesy Pork Ragu Pasta

Servings: 4 | Prep time: 10 minutes | Cooking time: 30 minutes

500g lean pork mince

1 onion, finely diced

1 carrot, finely diced

2 peppers, finely diced

2 cloves of garlic, finely grated

1 tbsp garlic granules

1 tbsp tomato purée

1 tbsp tarragon

½ tbsp basil

500g passata

1 chicken stock pot or cube

300g pasta

120g grated cheese (I use a combination of cheddar, mozzarella, and Red Leicester)

In a large pan, fry off the pork mince until browned.

Add the onion, carrot, and peppers to the pan. Cook until soft, then stir in the grated garlic.

Cook for another minute or so and then add the garlic granules, tomato purée, tarragon, and basil.

Mix well to combine all the ingredients, then add the passata and stock pot or cube.

Cook for at least 20 minutes, longer if you have time.

Meanwhile, put the pasta into a pan of boiling water with plenty of salt.

One the pasta is cooked, drain and add it to the ragu. Transfer the mixture to an ovenproof dish and top with the grated cheese.

Pop it under the grill until golden and bubbling. Serve and enjoy.

Tips: This ragu also works well in a lasagne. To make this, just swap out the pasta for lasagne sheets and follow the steps above. For a tasty béchamel sauce for the lasagne, follow the instructions on page 136.

CALORIES 452 PER PORTION

This fish pie dinner always reminds me of my childhood. My mum makes the best fish pie, so this is a take on hers but with a crispy filo top.

Filo-Topped Fish Pie

Servings: 4 | Prep time: 10 minutes | Cooking time: 30 minutes

2 onions, finely diced

1 tsp salt

1 tbsp oil

3 tbsp plain flour

200ml milk, warmed

200ml chicken stock

80g extra mature cheddar

1 tsp mustard (optional)

Salt and pepper, to taste

400g fish pie mix (I used salmon, cod and smoked haddock)

3-4 sheets of filo pastry

Cooking oil spray

Preheat the oven to 200°c/180°c fan.

Meanwhile, in a large pan, season the onions with salt and cook in the oil until soft. Stir in the flour and cook for another couple of minutes.

Slowly add the milk and chicken stock bit by bit, stirring continuously.

Once you have a thick sauce, add the cheese and mustard if using. Stir until the cheese has melted, then season with salt and pepper to taste.

Add the fish to the sauce, mix well, and cook gently for 5 minutes.

Put the fish pie mix into an ovenproof dish.

Scrunch the filo pastry up and place on top of the fish pie mix, spraying the top with a little cooking oil.

Pop this in the oven for 10-15 minutes or until piping hot, golden, and cooked through.

Serve and enjoy.

Tips: I like to serve this dish with mashed potato and greens. If you prefer, you can top this pie with mashed potato instead of the filo pastry.

I first made this for dinner a couple of years ago when my children decided they didn't like cottage pie anymore. This new version soon changed their minds and they even asked for seconds! The recipe includes all the flavours of a cheeseburger but in a comforting winter warmer.

Cheeseburger Cottage Pie

Servings: 4 | Prep time: 10 minutes | Cooking time: 1 hour

1 onion, finely diced

2 carrots, finely diced

2 cloves of garlic, finely grated

500g 5% fat beef mince

1 tsp each salt and pepper

2 tbsp ketchup

1 tbsp tomato purée

1 tbsp mustard

400ml beef stock

800g potatoes, peeled and chopped

4 large gherkins

4 tsp beef gravy granules (optional)

4 light cheese slices

50ml milk

1 tbsp light butter

60g grated cheese (I use a mixure of cheddar, mozzarella, and Red Leicester)

1 tbsp burger sauce (optional)

In a large pan, cook the diced onion and carrot in a little oil until soft.

Add the garlic to the pan and fry for another minute or so, then add the beef mince and the salt and pepper.

Once the beef mince has browned, add the ketchup, tomato purée, and mustard. Mix well until all the ingredients are combined.

Pour in the beef stock and then leave to cook on a low heat for at least 30 minutes, longer if you have time. Preheat the oven to 200°c/180°c fan.

Meanwhile, use another pan to boil the potatoes in salted water.

Once the beef is tender, dice 2 of the gherkins and stir them in. If you would like the sauce to be a little thicker, stir in the gravy granules too.

Put the beef mixture into an ovenproof dish and top with the cheese slices. Slice the remaining gherkins and lay these on top too.

Drain the potatoes and then mash them with the milk and butter.

Spoon the mash over the cheeseburger mix in the dish, spreading it out to form a level surface, then sprinkle with the grated cheese.

Place the dish in the preheated oven for 20 minutes, or until piping hot and the cheese is golden and bubbling.

Drizzle with the burger sauce if using. Serve and enjoy.

Cauliflower cheese has always been a staple side dish for a roast dinner. In this recipe, roasting the cauliflower and topping the dish with crispy breadcrumbs takes it to a whole new level.

Roasted Cauliflower Cheese

Servings: 4 | Prep time: 5 minutes | Cooking time: 40 minutes

1 cauliflower

1 tbsp oil

Salt and pepper

2 tbsp light butter

2 tbsp plain flour

300ml milk, warmed

2 tsp English mustard (optional)

120g grated extra mature cheddar

For the garlic and rosemary breadcrumbs

2 slices of bread

1 tsp rosemary

1 tbsp garlic granules

1 tbsp chopped fresh parsley

1 tbsp light butter

Tips: If you wanted to make this dish without roasting the cauliflower, you can parboil or steam it instead for around 5-6 minutes until tender, then skip straight to Step 3.

Preheat the oven to 220°c/200°c fan or an air fryer to 180°c.

Cut the cauliflower into florets and cover with the oil in an ovenproof dish. Season and place in the oven for 20 minutes.

Meanwhile, melt the butter in a saucepan and then add the flour. Mix well until it forms a paste (known as a roux). Slowly add the warmed milk bit by bit, stirring continuously.

Once you have a thick sauce, add the mustard (if using) and half the cheese. Mix well until the cheese has melted, then season to taste.

When the roasted cauliflower is ready, cover it with the cheese sauce and sprinkle over the remaining grated cheese.

Place the dish back into the oven for another 20 minutes.

Meanwhile, make the breadcrumb topping. Blitz the bread in a food processor to make fine crumbs, then stir in the rosemary, garlic and parsley.

In a clean frying pan, melt the butter and then fry the breadcrumbs until crispy and golden. Pour into a bowl and set aside.

Remove the cauliflower cheese from the oven and sprinkle the breadcrumbs over the top for a delicious crunch. Serve and enjoy.

20 MINUTE AND UNDER MEALS

This is my take on crispy chilli beef, using beef mince instead of the usual strips, and it works so well. Perfect for a Friday night fakeaway or even a quick midweek stir-fry.

Easy Crispy Chilli Beef Mince

Servings: 4 | Prep time: 5 minutes | Cooking time: 15 minutes

2 tbsp oil

500g lean beef mince

½ tbsp Chinese five spice

1 tbsp garlic granules

Pinch of salt

1 tsp chilli flakes

1 spring onion, sliced

2 peppers, finely diced

3 cloves of garlic, finely grated

5cm cube of root ginger, finely grated

Sesame seeds, chilli, and spring onion to garnish

For the sauce

2 tbsp sweet chilli sauce

1 tbsp rice wine vinegar

1 tbsp dark soy sauce

1 tbsp light soy sauce

1 tbsp ketchup

1 tbsp honey

Heat the oil in a pan until it's very hot and then add the beef mince. Stir in the five spice, garlic granules and salt.

Once the beef has browned, add the chilli flakes (using more or less to taste) along with the spring onion, peppers, garlic, and ginger.

Cook for a few minutes, being careful not to burn the garlic, then add all the sauce ingredients. Stir until the beef is fully cooked and the mixture is sticky and crispy.

Garnish with more sliced spring onion, sesame seeds and fresh chilli or chilli flakes according to your preference, then serve and enjoy.

Tips: This dish is so versatile and can be served in so many ways. We like it with rice, but you can also serve it with noodles, in a stir-fry with extra veggies, or even in a wrap.

What's not to love about this dinner? After it went viral on both Instagram and TikTok, I knew it had to be in my first cookbook. It only takes 10 minutes to make and is packed full of flavour. A winner!

Cajun Halloumi and Chorizo Pasta

Servings: 4 | Prep time: 2 minutes | Cooking time: 8 minutes

300g pasta
50g chorizo, diced
140g light halloumi, diced
½ tbsp smoked paprika
½ tbsp garlic granules
1-2 tbsp Cajun spice (or to taste)
3 cloves of garlic, finely grated
1 tbsp tomato purée
120ml light single cream
Salt and pepper, to taste
1 tsp chilli flakes (optional)
Fresh parsley, to garnish (optional)

Put the pasta into a pan of boiling water with plenty of salt.

Meanwhile, fry off the chorizo and halloumi with the seasonings until browned and getting crispy, then stir in the garlic and tomato purée.

Cook for another few minutes and then add the cream and drained cooked pasta.

Mix well, adding a little pasta water until you get the perfect consistency.

Season to taste with salt and pepper. If you like, garnish with some chilli flakes and fresh parsley.

Serve and enjoy.

Tips: Remember to get the water boiling for the pasta before you start prepping the other ingredients to save time.

My little girl, Lottie, absolutely loves spaghetti and meatballs, so this always goes down well with her. It's a quick and easy dinner too and can be achieved in just 20 minutes: perfect after a busy day.

Creamy Pesto Spaghetti and Meatballs

Servings: 4 | Prep time: 5 minutes | Cooking time: 15 minutes

20 small meatballs (approximately)

300g spaghetti

1 red onion, finely diced

2 cloves of garlic, grated

1 tbsp tomato purée

4 tbsp pesto (red or green)

200ml hot chicken stock

120ml light single cream

Salt and pepper, to taste

60g cheddar, finely grated

Fresh basil, to garnish

Start by frying the meatballs in a large pan for around 10 minutes.

Meanwhile, put the spaghetti into a pan of boiling water with a generous amount of salt.

Add the onion to the pan with the meatballs and cook until soft.

Stir in the garlic and cook for another minute.

Add the tomato purée and pesto to the pan and cook for another minute or so.

Pour in the stock and cream, then allow the sauce to reduce.

Once the meatballs are cooked through, check the seasoning and adjust as needed, then add the spaghetti to the meatballs along with a little pasta water to loosen the sauce.

Give this a good mix, adding more pasta water until you get the perfect silky consistency.

Garnish with the grated cheese and fresh basil. Serve and enjoy.

Tips: For an alternative to shop-bought meatballs, you can always use sausage meat rolled into little balls, or even make your own meatballs from scratch.

This is the perfect Saturday night dinner! All the flavour of a takeaway with a fraction of the calories.

Sweet Chilli Chicken

Servings: 4 | Prep time: 5 minutes | Cooking time: 10 minutes

500g chicken breast, diced

25g cornflour

1 tsp salt

1 tsp black pepper

Cooking oil spray

4 tbsp sweet chilli sauce

4 tbsp ketchup

1 tbsp light soy sauce

2 tsp ginger purée

2 tsp garlic purée

Sesame seeds (optional)

Sliced chilli and spring onion, to garnish (optional)

Preheat the oven to 240°c/220°c fan or an air fryer to 200°c.

In a bowl, coat the diced chicken in the cornflour, salt and pepper.

Spray the chicken with the oil and pop into the oven or air fryer for 10-15 minutes until cooked through and crispy on the outside.

Meanwhile, mix the sweet chilli sauce, ketchup, soy sauce, and purées together in a small pan and reduce to a sticky sauce.

Add the chicken to the pan and coat with the sauce, then transfer to a serving dish.

Garnish with the sesame seeds, chilli, and spring onion if using. Serve and enjoy.

Tips: We like to serve this with rice for dinner, but you could also serve it with noodles or stir-fried vegetables.

This recipe is in no way a traditional pasta dish, but wow is it tasty! The BBQ sauce is subtle but gives the dish that smoky BBQ flavour, without being too overpowering.

Creamy BBQ Bacon and Halloumi Spaghetti

Servings: 4 | Prep time: 2 minutes | Cooking time: 10 minutes

300g spaghetti

140g light halloumi, diced

150g bacon, diced

1 tbsp smoked paprika

1 tbsp garlic granules

½ tbsp paprika

½ tbsp oregano

Salt, to taste

2 cloves of garlic, finely grated

1 tbsp tomato purée

2 tbsp BBQ sauce, plus extra to serve

300ml chicken stock

120ml light single cream

60g cheddar, finely grated

Fresh parsley, to garnish (optional)

Place the spaghetti in a pan of boiling water with plenty of salt.

Fry off the halloumi and bacon in a large frying pan. Add the smoked paprika, garlic granules, paprika, oregano and salt.

Once the halloumi and bacon are browned, add the grated garlic.

Cook for a minute, then add the tomato purée and BBQ sauce. Mix well so that the halloumi and bacon are coated in the sauce. Cook for another minute or so.

Add the chicken stock and cream to the pan, stir well, then reduce the sauce on a low heat.

Add the cooked pasta with a few tablespoons of pasta water, then continue to cook while tossing or stirring until it forms a silky sauce.

Sprinkle over some grated cheese, then garnish with parsley and an extra drizzle of BBQ sauce if you like. Serve and enjoy.

Tips: Cook your spaghetti for 2 minutes less than it says on the packet; this way it stays perfectly al dente when served.

What's not to love about this dish? My kids will eat anything if it resembles pizza, so this is always a winner in my house.

Pizza Pasta

Servings: 4 | Prep time: 5 minutes | Cooking time: 15 minutes

300g short pasta
20 slices of pepperoni
1 red onion, finely diced
2 peppers, finely diced
2 cloves of garlic, finely grated
1 tbsp tomato purée
1 tbsp oregano
500g passata
1 tsp salt, or to taste
80g grated mozzarella

Start by putting the pasta on to boil in a pan of water with plenty of salt.

Cut half the pepperoni slices into quarters and leave the other half whole. Fry the quartered pepperoni in a large pan.

When the oils are released and the pepperoni is starting to go crispy, add the onion and peppers. Cook until soft and then add the garlic.

Add the tomato purée to the pan and cook for another few minutes.

Stir in the oregano and passata, cook for 3-4 minutes, then season with the salt.

Add the cooked pasta to the pan and mix well. Transfer the mixture to an ovenproof dish and top with the grated cheese and remaining pepperoni slices.

Pop it under a hot grill until the cheese has melted and the pepperoni is crisp.

Serve and enjoy.

Tips: You can personalise this dish with any of your favourite pizza toppings, such as extra veggies like mushrooms and sweetcorn.

This is such a quick and easy dinner, perfect for the end of a busy day when you don't want to spend too long in the kitchen. I love the smoky flavour of harissa and it goes so well with pasta.

Creamy Harissa Spaghetti

Servings: 4 | Prep time: 2 minutes | Cooking time: 10 minutes

300g spaghetti

400g sausages (approx. 8)

1 tbsp smoked paprika

½ tbsp oregano

1 onion, finely diced

2 cloves of garlic, finely grated

1 tbsp tomato purée

1 tbsp harissa, or to taste

120ml light single cream

Salt and pepper, to taste

Fresh parsley and chilli flakes, to garnish (optional)

Put the spaghetti into a pan of boiling water with plenty of salt to cook until al dente.

Take the sausage meat out of the skins and break up into pieces. Put the pieces in a large frying pan to cook.

Once they've started to brown, add the smoked paprika and oregano.

Mix well, then add the onion and cook until soft.

Stir in the garlic and tomato purée to cook for a minute or two.

Add the harissa and cream and mix well to combine all the ingredients.

Add the cooked pasta along with some pasta water if needed, and stir until it's the perfect consistency.

Season with salt and pepper to taste, then garnish with some parsley and chilli flakes if using. Serve and enjoy.

Tips: You can swap out the sausage as the protein in this dish for anything else you fancy. The dish would work well with chicken, bacon, tofu, or halloumi.

Tuna pasta bake is a classic for a reason. Melted cheese and a rich tomato sauce make this dish super delicious. It's also amazing the next day for packed lunches.

Tuna Pasta Bake

Servings: 4 | Prep time: 12 minutes | Cooking time: 15 minutes

300g pasta

1 onion, finely diced

2 cloves of garlic, finely grated

1 tsp dried rosemary

1 tbsp tomato purée

1 tbsp white wine vinegar

500g passata

1 chicken stock pot or cube

2 tins of tuna, drained

120g grated cheddar

Put the pasta on to boil in a pan of water with plenty of salt.

In another large pan, cook the onion until soft, then add the garlic and rosemary.

Cook for another minute or so and then add the tomato purée and white wine vinegar.

Mix well and then add the passata and stock pot or crumbled cube.

Cook for around 5 minutes and then add the tuna to the pan, mixing well.

Fold the cooked pasta into the sauce, then place this mixture into an ovenproof dish.

Top with the grated cheese, then pop it under a hot grill until golden and bubbling.

Serve and enjoy.

Tips: I like to use tuna in either spring water or brine. Try to avoid tuna in oil as it contains more calories.

The fragrance of the garlic and ginger, with the kick of chilli, works so well with the sweetness of the juicy prawns. This quick and easy dinner is bound to become a new favourite.

Garlic, Chilli and Ginger Prawn Linguine

Serving: 4 | Prep time: 2 minutes | Cooking time: 10 minutes

300g linguine

1 tbsp olive oil

2 tbsp light butter

6 cloves of garlic, finely sliced

2 tsp chilli flakes, or to taste

2 tsp ginger purée

400g raw prawns

½ lemon, juiced

2 tbsp chopped fresh parsley

½ tsp salt, or to taste

Red chilli, sliced (optional)

Parsley, finely chopped

Put the linguine into a pan of boiling water with plenty of salt to cook.

Splash the oil into a large pan and add the butter. Melt on a medium heat, then add the garlic, chilli and ginger purée.

Mix well and cook on a low heat for a few minutes, being careful not to burn the garlic.

Turn the heat up and pop in the prawns. Cook for a minute or so until the prawns are pink throughout.

Stir the lemon juice and parsley into the prawns, then add the cooked and drained linguine.

Pour in a little pasta water if needed to create a lovely sauce that coats the pasta and prawns.

Season to taste with salt, garnish with finely chopped parsley and sliced red chilli then serve and enjoy.

Tips: I buy the prawns already prepared to save on time, but if you choose to buy yours fresh, make sure to take the intestinal tract out along the back of each prawn, which isn't very pleasant to eat.

If you're looking for a quick and easy dinner idea, then look no further. This spicy sausage pasta ticks all the boxes; it's incredibly delicious and takes less than 20 minutes to make!

Spicy Sausage Pasta

Servings: 4 | Prep time: 2 minutes | Cooking time: 15 minutes

8 sausages, skinned

1 tbsp smoked paprika

300g pasta of your choice

2 cloves of garlic, finely grated

1 tsp chilli flakes

2 tbsp tomato purée

1 tbsp white wine vinegar

300ml chicken stock

120ml light single cream

Chilli flakes and fresh parsley, to garnish

Break up the sausage meat into small pieces, then brown them in a pan with the smoked paprika.

Meanwhile, put the pasta on to boil in a pan of salted water.

Once the sausages are cooked, add the garlic and chilli flakes, then cook for another minute.

Add the tomato purée and white wine vinegar to the sausages, mix well and cook for another few minutes.

Pour the chicken stock and cream into the pan, then reduce until you have a thicker sauce.

Now add the cooked pasta with a little pasta water and mix well until combined.

Garnish with the chilli flakes and parsley to taste.

Serve and enjoy.

Tips: If you don't have time to take the sausages out their skins, you can just chop them up instead.

This simple summery dish is so quick that you can cook it in the time it takes to boil the pasta.

Lemon and Garlic Salmon Spaghetti

Servings: 4 | Prep time: 2 minutes | Cooking time: 10 minutes

300g spaghetti

2 salmon fillets

1 tbsp light butter

3 cloves of garlic, finely grated

½ lemon, juiced

1 tbsp plain flour

400ml chicken or fish stock

120ml light single cream

Salt and pepper, to taste

Handful of chives, to garnish

Put your spaghetti on to boil in a pan of water with plenty of salt.

Meanwhile, generously season the salmon and then fry it in a large pan for 5-6 minutes, turning the fillets over halfway through and adding the butter to the pan near the end.

Once cooked, remove the salmon from the pan and set aside to rest. Leave the melted butter in the pan.

Add the garlic to the butter and cook for a minute or two (being careful not to let it brown). Add the lemon juice to the pan, then add the flour and cook out for a minute or so.

Slowly pour the stock into the pan, stirring continuously to make a smooth sauce.

Lower the heat right down and add the cream, then flake the cooked salmon into the sauce. Mix well, gently so you don't break up the salmon too much, then season to taste.

Add the cooked spaghetti and a little pasta water to the pan, tossing until coated.

Finish with some chopped chives to serve and enjoy.

Tips: You can swap out the single cream for either cream cheese or crème fraiche if you prefer.

If you like a little bit of spice then you'll love this creamy nduja spaghetti, which is delicious and takes no time at all to make. The perfect midweek meal.

Nduja and Halloumi Spaghetti

Servings: 4 | Prep time: 2 minutes | Cooking time: 10 minutes

300g spaghetti

140g light halloumi, diced

1 tbsp smoked paprika

2 cloves of garlic, finely grated

2 tbsp nduja paste

200ml chicken stock

120ml light single cream

Chilli flakes and fresh parsley, to garnish

Put the spaghetti on to boil with plenty of salt.

Fry the halloumi with the smoked paprika in a large frying pan.

Once the halloumi has browned, add the garlic and stir well.

Cook for a minute, then add the nduja paste and cook for another minute or so.

Add the chicken stock and cream, stirring well, then let the liquid reduce a little.

Add the cooked pasta and some pasta water to the pan. Toss to combine and cook until it forms a silky sauce.

Transfer the spaghetti to a warm serving dish, then garnish with chilli flakes and parsley.

Serve and enjoy.

Tips: You can swap out the halloumi for any other type of protein you like. If you add chicken as well as halloumi to the dish, it takes the calories per portion to 595.

Simple yet so full of flavour, this is the perfect quick and easy dinner for those busy midweek days.

Pesto and Mozzarella Pork

Servings: 4 | Prep time: 2 minutes | Cooking time: 18 minutes

4 pork steaks

Salt and pepper

4 tbsp pesto (red or green)

125g mozzarella ball, drained and sliced

Preheat the oven to 220°c/200°c fan or an air fryer to 180°c.

Season the pork steaks with salt and pepper, then top each steak with a tablespoon of pesto and cover with the mozzarella slices.

Cook for around 15-20 minutes in the oven or air fryer until the pork is cooked through.

Serve and enjoy with sides of your choice.

Tips: We like mash and greens with these pork steaks, but they would also be amazing with some crispy potato wedges and a fresh salad.

What's not to love about this kind of dinner: quick, easy, and very delicious. Spicy and smoky Cajun in a rich tomato sauce with a perfectly cheesy top. Heaven!

Cajun Sausage and Tomato Pasta

Servings: 4 | Prep time: 2 minutes | Cooking time: 15 minutes

300g pasta
8 sausages, chopped
1 onion, finely diced
2 cloves of garlic, finely grated
1 tbsp Cajun seasoning
1 tbsp smoked paprika
1 tbsp tomato purée
1 tbsp white wine vinegar
500g passata
1 chicken stock pot or cube
120g cheddar, grated

Put the pasta into a pan of boiling water with plenty of salt to cook.

Meanwhile, fry the sausages in a pan until browned and then add the onion.

Once the onions are soft, stir in the garlic, Cajun seasoning and paprika.

Cook for another minute or so and then add the tomato purée and white wine vinegar.

Mix well and then add the passata and stock pot or cube.

Cook for about 5 minutes and then mix in the cooked pasta. Transfer the mixture to an ovenproof dish, then top with the grated cheese.

Pop it under a hot grill until golden and bubbling.

Serve and enjoy.

Tips: If you like things a little spicier, add more Cajun seasoning to give the sauce an extra kick. Perhaps even add some chilli flakes if you like it hot!

Pasta salads are one of my favourite meals to cook in the summertime. This recipe has to be one of my all-time favourites. Full of flavour and so filling, it's great for meal prep and for packed lunches too.

Chicken, Chorizo and Halloumi Pasta Salad

Servings: 4 | Prep time: 5 minutes | Cooking time: 15 minutes

For the pasta salad

50g chorizo, diced

500g chicken breast, diced

1 tbsp smoked paprika

1 tbsp garlic granules

½ tbsp oregano

300g pasta

100g light halloumi, diced

½ cucumber, diced

2 red peppers, diced

1 red onion, finely diced

For the harissa dressing

4 tbsp fat-free natural yoghurt

4 tbsp mayonnaise

½ lemon, juiced

2 cloves of garlic, finely chopped

1 tbsp harissa, or to taste

In a frying pan, fry the chorizo until crisp. Remove from the pan and set aside, leaving the chorizo oil in the pan.

In the same pan, cook the chicken with the paprika, garlic granules and oregano for 7-10 minutes.

Meanwhile, add the pasta to a pan of boiling water with plenty of salt. Once the pasta is cooked, drain and rinse it under the cold tap to cool.

When the chicken is nearly cooked through, add the diced halloumi and cook until browned.

For the dressing, simply mix the yoghurt, mayonnaise, lemon juice, garlic, and harissa in a bowl. Season with salt to taste.

Combine the cooled pasta, chicken and halloumi mixture, crispy chorizo, diced cucumber, peppers, and onion in a large bowl.

Drizzle the dressing over the pasta salad, give it a good mix, then serve and enjoy.

Tips: If you'd prefer this recipe without any spice, you can leave the harissa out of the dressing to make it less spicy.

Quick dinners are a must in this house! This recipe is perfect for that as it only takes 12 minutes from start to finish, while still tasting amazing.

Bacon, Halloumi and Pesto Spaghetti

Servings: 4 | Prep time: 2 minutes | Cooking time: 10 minutes

300g spaghetti

150g light halloumi, diced

150g bacon, diced

2 cloves of garlic, finely grated

1 tbsp tomato purée

½ jar of reduced-fat pesto (red or green)

120ml light single cream

Fresh parsley or basil, to garnish (optional)

Put the spaghetti into a pan of boiling water with plenty of salt to cook.

Meanwhile, fry off the halloumi and bacon in a large frying pan until browned.

Once browned, stir in the garlic and tomato purée.

Cook for a minute and then add the pesto and cream along with a ladle full of the pasta cooking water. Cook for another minute or so.

Add the cooked and drained spaghetti, stir well, and cook until a silky sauce forms, adding more pasta water if needed.

If you like, garnish with some parsley or basil.

Serve and enjoy.

Tips: Start prepping the ingredients while you wait for the pasta water to boil; that way you're saving even more time!

ONE POT WONDERS

I first made this dish back in March 2022 and it's been a favourite both in my house and online ever since. So many of you have made it and gotten in touch to say how much you loved it, so I knew that it had to make an appearance in my first cookbook.

One Pot Piri-Piri Chicken and Halloumi Rice

Servings: 4 | Prep time: 5 minutes | Cooking time: 20 minutes

500g chicken, diced

1 tbsp piri-piri seasoning

1 onion, finely diced

2 peppers, finely diced

2 cloves of garlic, finely grated

1 tsp ground turmeric

1 tsp smoked paprika

1 tsp salt

4 tbsp Nando's Marinade

250g basmati rice

600ml chicken stock

60g grated cheddar

120g halloumi, sliced

Chilli jam, to taste

Nando's Perinaise

In a large frying pan that has a lid, fry the chicken with half the piri-piri seasoning.

Once browned, take the chicken out and set aside for later.

In the same pan, fry the onion and peppers until soft. Add the garlic, remaining piri-piri seasoning, turmeric, smoked paprika, and salt.

Add the chicken back to the pan, along with the Nando's Marinade and the uncooked basmati rice.

Mix well and then add the chicken stock. Place the lid on the pan and cook on a low heat for about 20 minutes or until the rice is fully cooked, adding more liquid if needed.

Once cooked, transfer the mixture to an ovenproof dish, sprinkle with the cheddar and top with the sliced halloumi.

Place it under a hot grill, turning the halloumi slices halfway through so they turn golden on both sides. Alternatively, you can fry the halloumi in the pan if you prefer.

Drizzle with the chilli jam and Nando's Perinaise to taste, then serve and enjoy.

Tips: I like to use the lemon and herb flavour of Nando's Marinade, but you can use any flavour that you like. You can also reduce the amount of piri-piri seasoning if you don't like too much spice and want to make the dish a little tamer.

Dinners like this chicken traybake make me so happy. You can just pop it all in the oven and get on with other things while it cooks.

Hunter's Chicken Traybake

Servings: 4 | Prep time: 5 minutes | Cooking time: 40 minutes

800g potatoes

3 peppers, sliced

1 red onion, sliced

600g skinless and boneless chicken thighs

2 cloves of garlic, finely grated

2 tbsp smoked paprika

1 tbsp BBQ seasoning

1 tbsp garlic granules

½ tsp salt

6 rashers of streaky bacon, halved

80g grated cheddar

4 tbsp BBQ sauce

Fresh parsley, to garnish

Preheat the oven to 220°c/200°c fan or an air fryer to 180°c.

Peel the potatoes and then chop into even wedges so they're all similar in size.

Put the wedges into a large ovenproof dish along with the peppers, onion, chicken thighs, grated garlic, smoked paprika, BBQ seasoning, garlic granules and salt.

Mix it all together and place into the oven or air fryer for 30 minutes. After this time, add the bacon, grated cheddar and BBQ sauce on top of the chicken thighs to cover them evenly.

Cook for another 10 minutes or until the chicken and potatoes are cooked through.

Garnish with some fresh parsley, then serve and enjoy.

Tips: If you'd prefer to use chicken breasts instead of chicken thighs, cook the potatoes for 10 minutes before adding the chicken, as chicken breasts will take less time to cook than thighs.

CALORIES
626
PER
PORTION

Orzo will always have my heart and cooking it all in one pot gives it a smooth, creamy finish, similar to a risotto. This is definitely a must try!

One Pot Chicken, Bacon and Mozzarella Orzo

Servings: 4 | Prep time: 5 minutes | Cooking time: 20 minutes

500g chicken, diced
150g smoked bacon, diced
1 tbsp smoked paprika
1 tbsp garlic granules
½ tbsp oregano
1 tsp salt
1 onion, finely diced
2 peppers, finely diced
3 cloves of garlic, minced
1 tbsp tomato purée
300g orzo
1 litre hot chicken stock
60g mozzarella
Fresh parsley, to garnish

Start by cooking the chicken, bacon, seasonings, and salt in a large frying pan until browned.

Add the onion and peppers, then stir in the garlic once they have softened and cook for another minute. Add the tomato purée and mix well.

Stir in the orzo and then add the stock bit by bit until the orzo is cooked. You may not need the full litre of stock. Keep stirring so nothing sticks to the bottom.

Once the orzo is cooked, tear in half the mozzarella and stir until melted. Tear the remaining mozzarella over the top and pop the dish under a hot grill until golden and bubbling.

Garnish with the fresh parsley, then serve and enjoy.

Tips: If you'd prefer this dish without meat you can always swap the chicken and bacon for plant-based alternatives, or halloumi also works well here.

Steak and peppercorn sauce is a classic combination that everybody knows and loves. This one pot wonder has all those flavours and more in the most delicious pasta dish.

Cheesy Peppercorn Steak Pasta

Servings: 4 | Prep time: 5 minutes | Cooking time: 20 minutes

2 steaks

1 onion, finely diced

3 peppers, finely diced

1 tbsp crushed peppercorns

300g pasta

600ml milk, warmed

600ml beef stock

120g grated cheese (I use a mix of cheddar and mozzarella)

Salt and pepper, to taste

Fresh parsley, to garnish

Season the steaks generously with salt and pepper, then fry them in a large pan until cooked to your liking. Once done, take the steaks out of the pan and set aside to rest.

In the same pan, cook the onion and peppers until they start to soften. Add the crushed peppercorns and a pinch of salt. Cook for a further minute or two.

Add the pasta, milk and stock to the pan of onion and peppers and stir well. Cook for about 15 minutes on a medium heat until the pasta is fully cooked, adding more liquid if needed.

Slice the steak and add this to the pan along with half the grated cheese. Mix well and preheat your grill to a high setting.

Transfer the mixture to an ovenproof dish and sprinkle with the remaining cheese. Place the dish under the hot grill until golden and bubbling. Garnish with fresh parsley to taste.

Serve and enjoy.

Tips: I like to use a lean rump steak for this dish, but you can use any cut of steak you prefer. Rib-eye works well too, but it is a little fattier.

This dinner really doesn't need much of an introduction; the combination of pesto in a creamy sauce with the smoky chorizo is a thing of beauty.

One Pot Creamy Pesto Pasta with Chicken and Chorizo

Servings: 4 | Prep time: 2 minutes | Cooking time: 20 minutes

50g chorizo, diced

500g chicken breast, diced

1 tbsp smoked paprika

1 tbsp garlic granules

½ tbsp basil

1 tsp salt

1 red onion, diced

2 red peppers, diced

1 tbsp tomato purée

4 tbsp pesto (red or green)

300g pasta

1 litre chicken stock

120ml single light cream

Fresh basil, to garnish (optional)

Fry the chorizo in a large pan until the edges are crispy and the oils have started to come out, then remove from the pan and set aside.

In the same pan, fry the chicken in all the seasoning and salt until it starts to brown. Add the onion and peppers and cook until soft.

Stir in the tomato purée and pesto, cook for a minute or two, then add the uncooked pasta along with half the stock.

Let it simmer and stir occasionally, adding more stock when needed. Once the stock has been soaked up and the pasta is cooked, add the cream.

Give the dish a good mix, season to taste and then garnish with fresh basil leaves if you like. Serve and enjoy.

Tips: You can use any pesto for this recipe. If you're not keen on green pesto, red pesto and red pepper pesto both work really well.

A delicious buffalo chicken orzo that is so easy and all cooked in one pot. What more could you want?

One Pot Buffalo Chicken Orzo

Servings: 4 | Prep time: 5 minutes | Cooking time: 25 minutes

500g chicken breast, diced

1 tbsp smoked paprika

1 tbsp garlic granules

½ tbsp oregano

1 tsp salt

1 onion, finely diced

2 cloves of garlic, finely grated

1 tbsp tomato purée

8 tbsp buffalo sauce

300g orzo

1 litre chicken stock

120ml light single cream

4 tbsp ranch dressing

Fresh parsley, to garnish

Start by seasoning the diced chicken with the paprika, garlic, oregano, and salt in a bowl, tossing until all the pieces are evenly coated. Now fry the chicken in a frying pan until it starts to brown.

Add the onions and cook until soft, then stir in the grated garlic and cook for a few minutes, being careful not to let it brown.

Add the tomato purée and buffalo sauce, cook for another minute, then add the uncooked orzo.

Mix it all together and then add the chicken stock in two parts, stirring until all the liquid has been absorbed and the orzo is cooked.

Pour in the cream and give the orzo a good mix.

Garnish with the ranch dressing and fresh parsley, then serve and enjoy.

Tips: You can swap the ranch dressing for a blue cheese dressing if you prefer. The calories would be 573 if you decided to make this swap.

Cheesy pasta has got to be one of the most comforting meals out there! Creamy, cheesy, and a little bit spicy with a delicious crunchy breadcrumb topping, this dish has it all.

One Pot Cheesy Cajun Chicken Macaroni

Servings: 4 | Prep time: 5 minutes | Cooking time: 20 minutes

500g chicken breast

1-2 tbsp Cajun seasoning

1 tbsp smoked paprika

1 tbsp garlic granules

1 onion, finely diced

2 peppers, finely diced

3 cloves of garlic, finely grated

300g macaroni

500ml chicken stock

500ml semi-skimmed milk, warmed

120g grated cheese (I use a mix of cheddar and mozzarella)

1 tsp mustard (optional)

Salt and pepper

Fresh coriander and chilli, to garnish

For the breadcrumb topping

2 slices of bread

1 tbsp Cajun seasoning

½ tsp salt

1 tbsp light butter

Start by frying the chicken with all the seasonings in a large pan until it begins to turn brown.

Add the onion and peppers to the pan and cook until soft, then add the garlic and fry for a further minute or so.

Add the uncooked pasta to the pan, give it a good mix and then add the stock and milk.

Cook for about 15-20 minutes until the pasta is fully cooked, adding more liquid gradually if needed.

Meanwhile, prepare the breadcrumb topping. Blitz the bread in a food processor to make fine crumbs, then stir in the Cajun seasoning and salt. In a clean frying pan, melt the butter and then fry the Cajun breadcrumbs until crispy and golden. Pour into a bowl and set aside.

Add half the cheese to the pan of pasta and stir until melted, then stir in the mustard if using and season with salt and pepper to taste.

Transfer the pasta into an ovenproof dish, then sprinkle the remaining cheese on top.

Place the dish under a hot grill until golden and bubbling. Top with the crispy Cajun breadcrumbs.

Garnish with the fresh coriander and chilli, then serve and enjoy.

This recipe is a dinner I've been making for years. I love the smoky flavours in this dish, and it is just so simple to make. It's perfect for a summer's evening, enjoyed in the garden with a glass of sangria.

Spanish Traybake

Servings: 4 | Prep time: 5 minutes | Cooking time: 40 minutes

500g baby potatoes

3 peppers, sliced

1 red onion, sliced

600g skinless and boneless chicken thighs

50g chorizo, sliced

3 cloves of garlic, finely grated

2 tbsp smoked paprika

1 tbsp ground coriander

1 tbsp garlic granules

½ tsp chilli flakes

½ tsp sugar or sweetener

½ tsp salt

4 tbsp light mayonnaise

Fresh parsley, to garnish

Preheat the oven to 220°c/200°c fan. Cut the baby potatoes evenly into quarters so that they're all similar in size.

Put the potatoes in a large ovenproof dish along with the peppers, onion, chicken thighs, chorizo, 2 cloves of garlic, all the seasonings, sugar, and salt.

Mix well and then place the dish into the oven for 40 minutes until the potatoes and chicken are cooked through.

While that's cooking, make the aioli by mixing the remaining clove of garlic into the mayonnaise along with a pinch of salt and a tiny bit of water, until it's a loose consistency.

Once the traybake is cooked, remove from the oven, and drizzle the aioli on top.

Garnish with some fresh parsley, then serve and enjoy.

Tips: This dinner is so delicious when served with crusty bread for mopping up all those juices. I buy the mini bake-at-home baguettes that are usually about 140 calories each.

One of my all-time favourites is chicken Kievs. When I made a one pot chicken Kiev pasta and posted the recipe on Instagram last year, you all loved it, so I've been working on version 2.0 and here it is! Garlicky, creamy, crunchy breadcrumbs… I think this may be my new favourite!

One Pot Creamy Chicken Kiev Orzo

Servings: 4 | Prep time: 5 minutes | Cooking time: 25 minutes

500g chicken breast, diced

1 tbsp garlic granules

½ tbsp parsley

1 tsp salt

1 onion, finely diced

5 cloves of garlic, finely grated

1 tbsp white wine vinegar

300g orzo

1 litre chicken stock

120ml light single cream

Fresh chives, to garnish

For the garlic breadcrumbs

2 slices of bread

1 tbsp garlic granules

½ tsp parsley

½ tsp salt

1 tbsp light butter

Start by seasoning the chicken with the garlic granules, parsley and salt. Fry it in a large frying pan until it starts to turn brown, then add the onions and cook until soft.

Add the garlic to the pan and cook for a few minutes, being careful not to let it brown.

Now add the white wine vinegar and cook for another minute before adding the uncooked orzo.

Mix it all together and then add the chicken stock in two parts until all the liquid has been absorbed and the orzo is cooked.

Meanwhile, make the garlic breadcrumb topping. Blitz the bread in a food processor to make fine crumbs, then stir in the garlic, parsley and salt. In a clean frying pan, melt the butter and then fry the garlic breadcrumbs until crispy and golden. Pour into a bowl and set aside.

Add the cream and chives to the pan of orzo and give it a good mix. Top with the crispy garlic breadcrumbs, then serve and enjoy.

Tips: If you'd prefer an alternative to cream here, you could always use cream cheese, crème fraiche or any other cream substitute instead.

Cajun seasoning might not be traditional with pasta, but it just works so well, especially with the addition of smoked paprika to give it that smoky, spicy kick.

One Pot Creamy Cajun Orzo

Servings: 4 | Prep time: 7 minutes | Cooking time: 20 minutes

500g chicken, diced

2 tbsp Cajun seasoning

1 tbsp smoked paprika

1 tbsp garlic granules

1 tsp salt

1 onion, finely diced

3 peppers, finely diced

2 cloves of garlic, finely grated

1 tbsp tomato purée

300g orzo

1 litre chicken stock

120ml light single cream

Fresh coriander and chilli, to garnish (optional)

Fry off the diced chicken in all the seasonings and salt until browned.

Add the onion and peppers to cook until soft.

Stir in the garlic and tomato purée and cook for a few minutes, then add the uncooked orzo and stir everything together.

Add the stock bit by bit, stirring occasionally, until the liquid has been absorbed and the orzo is cooked through.

Stir in the cream, then garnish with fresh coriander and chilli if you like. Serve and enjoy.

Tips: You can change the protein in this dish if you don't want to use chicken. You can either swap to a different meat, a meat-free alternative or just pack it with some extra veggies.

French onion soup has always been the first thing I order whenever I visit France. This macaroni cheese has all the flavours and textures of a French onion soup, combined in a delicious pasta dish.

One Pot French Onion Macaroni Cheese

Servings: 4 | Prep time: 5 minutes | Cooking time: 20 minutes

1 tbsp light butter

4 onions, thinly sliced

2 cloves of garlic, finely grated

2 tsp thyme

300g macaroni

500ml beef stock

500ml milk, warmed

120g grated cheese (I use a mix of cheddar and mozzarella)

1 tsp mustard (optional)

Salt and pepper

Fresh parsley, to garnish

For the onion breadcrumbs

2 slices of bread

1 tbsp onion granules

½ tsp salt

1 tbsp light butter

Start by melting the butter in a large pan and frying the onions until they're soft and caramelised. Add the garlic and thyme and mix well.

Cook for a few more minutes, then add the uncooked pasta, beef stock and milk.

Let this simmer for about 15-20 minutes until the pasta is fully cooked, gradually adding more liquid if needed.

Meanwhile, prepare the breadcrumb topping. Blitz the bread in a food processor to make fine crumbs, then stir in the onion granules and salt.

In a clean frying pan, melt the butter and then fry the onion breadcrumbs until crispy and golden. Pour into a bowl and set aside.

Add half the cheese to the pan of pasta and stir until melted, then stir in the mustard if using. Season with salt and pepper to taste.

Transfer the pasta into an ovenproof dish, then sprinkle the remaining cheese on top.

Place the dish under a hot grill until golden and bubbling. Top with the crispy onion breadcrumbs and fresh parsley, then serve and enjoy.

Tips: I always think a nice extra mature cheddar works best for this dish, as you don't need much to get a strong cheesy flavour.

This is one of my favourite meals to have on those days when it's too hot to cook. Just pop it all on a baking tray and leave to do its thing, then come back to a delicious dinner that everyone will enjoy.

Piri-Piri Chicken and Halloumi Traybake

Servings: 4 | Prep time: 5 minutes | Cooking time: 40 minutes

500g potatoes, peeled

3 peppers, sliced

1 red onion, sliced

600g skinless and boneless chicken thighs

2 cloves of garlic, finely grated

4 tbsp Nando's Marinade

1 tbsp piri-piri seasoning

½ tsp salt

150g light halloumi

2 tbsp chilli jam

80g grated cheddar

2 tbsp Nando's Perinaise

Fresh parsley, to garnish

Preheat the oven to 220°c/200°c fan.

Chop the potatoes into even wedges so they're all similar in size.

Put the wedges, peppers and onion into a large ovenproof dish along with the chicken thighs, garlic, Nando's Marinade, seasoning, and salt.

Mix it all together well and place in the oven for 30 minutes.

Meanwhile, brush the halloumi with some of the chilli jam.

After 30 minutes, take the dish out of the oven and top with the halloumi and cheddar.

Place back into the oven and cook for another 10 minutes or until the chicken and potatoes are cooked through.

Garnish with the Nando's Perinaise, fresh parsley and some extra chilli jam if you like.

Serve and enjoy.

Tips: If you're cooking for little ones who don't like a lot of spice, swap the piri-piri seasoning for smoked paprika or a generic chicken seasoning. You can also use a mild Nando's Marinade like the lemon and herb flavour.

This creamy, indulgent orzo recipe is a big family favourite. It was also a bit hit online, reaching two million people with thousands of you recreating it. The combination of smoky chorizo and creamy, garlicky Boursin cheese is always a winner.

One Pot Smoky Chorizo, Chicken and Boursin Orzo

Servings: 4 | Prep time: 5 minutes | Cooking time: 25 minutes

50g chorizo, sliced

500g chicken breast, diced

1 tbsp smoked paprika

½ tbsp each garlic granules, paprika, oregano & parsley

1 tsp salt

1 onion, finely diced

2 cloves of garlic, finely grated

1 tbsp white wine vinegar

1 tbsp tomato purée

300g orzo

1 litre hot chicken stock

100g Boursin

Handful of fresh chives, finely chopped

60g parmesan or cheddar, finely grated (optional)

Start by frying off the chorizo until nice and crisp, then remove it from the pan.

In the same pan, cook the chicken with all the spices, herbs and salt for a few minutes until browned.

Add the onion, then once softened stir in the garlic, white wine vinegar and tomato purée.

Cook for another few minutes and then add the uncooked orzo. Mix well and then add the stock bit by bit, stirring occasionally, until all the liquid has been soaked up and the orzo is cooked through.

Add the Boursin and mix well. Finish with the crispy chorizo, chives, and a sprinkle of cheese if you like. Serve and enjoy.

Tips: Prep everything before you start cooking, including measuring out all the herbs and spices. That way you have everything to hand, ready to be added when needed.

Chicken, chorizo, and Cajun spice go together so perfectly. The best thing about this dish is that you can pop it all in the oven and walk away until it's done, making it perfect for those busy days.

Cajun Chicken and Chorizo Traybake

Servings: 4 | Prep time: 5 minutes | Cooking time: 40 minutes

600g skinless and boneless chicken thighs

500g baby potatoes, quartered

50g chorizo, sliced

3 peppers, sliced

1 red onion, sliced

2 cloves of garlic, finely grated

2 tbsp Cajun seasoning

1 tbsp smoked paprika

4 tbsp light mayonnaise

1 tsp mint sauce

½ tsp salt (optional)

Fresh parsley (optional)

Preheat the oven to 220°c/200°c fan.

Place the chicken thighs, potatoes, chorizo, peppers, onion, and garlic into a large ovenproof dish along with the Cajun seasoning and paprika.

Mix well until all the ingredients are coated in the seasoning and then pop the dish into the oven for 30 minutes, or until the chicken and potatoes are cooked through.

Meanwhile, add the mayonnaise and mint sauce to a bowl and mix well until combined. If needed, add a few drops of water to get a looser consistency. Season with the salt if needed.

Remove the dish from the oven and drizzle the minted mayonnaise over the traybake.

Garnish with some fresh parsley. Serve and enjoy.

Tips: If you don't fancy Cajun as your spice, you can swap the seasoning for any that you prefer, such as garlic granules. Fajita seasoning also works really well too!

CALORIES **633** PER PORTION

I first made this dish in lockdown, when one of my friends mentioned a similar dish that she makes, and it has been a firm family favourite ever since. The flavours work so well together and best of all, there's less washing up with it all being made in one pot!

One Pot Cheesy Mexican Rice

Servings: 4 | Prep time: 5 minutes | Cooking time: 20 minutes

50g chorizo, diced

500g chicken, diced

1-2 tbsp fajita or taco seasoning

1 onion, finely diced

2 peppers, diced

2 cloves of garlic, grated

250g basmati rice

120ml light single cream

200ml milk, warmed

600ml chicken stock

120g grated cheese (I use a mix of cheddar, Red Leicester and mozzarella)

Salt and pepper

Fresh chilli and coriander, to garnish

Fry the chorizo in a frying pan until crisp, then remove and put to one side.

Add the chicken and the seasoning to the same pan and cook for around 5 minutes or until browned. Take the chicken out of the pan and put to one side.

In the same pan, cook the onion and peppers until they're soft, then add the garlic.

Cook for a few minutes and then add the chicken and chorizo back in, along with the uncooked rice, and mix well.

Once the rice is all mixed in, add the cream, milk and stock. Cook on a low heat with a lid on for about 10-15 minutes or until the rice is cooked through, adding more liquid if necessary. Try not to stir the rice as it will go stodgy. Instead, use a fork to fluff it up.

Once cooked, transfer the mix to an ovenproof dish. Season to taste with salt and pepper, then sprinkle the grated cheese on top.

Place the dish under the grill until bubbling and golden.

Garnish with the chilli and coriander, then serve and enjoy.

Tips: If you like a bit of spice, you can always add some chilli flakes for a little extra kick. I tend to sprinkle them on after serving so that it's not too spicy for my children.

CALORIES 516 PER PORTION

This meal contains all the best bits of a chicken Kiev but in an easy traybake. Anything with garlic, cheese and crunchy breadcrumbs is a winner in my eyes!

Cheesy Chicken Kiev Traybake

Servings: 4 | Prep time: 5 minutes | Cooking time: 40 minutes

800g baby potatoes

600g skinless and boneless chicken thighs

5 cloves of garlic, finely grated

1 tbsp parsley

½ tbsp thyme

1 tsp salt, or to taste

50g bread (approx. 2 small slices)

1 tbsp garlic granules

60g parmesan

½ tbsp chopped fresh parsley

Fresh parsley sprigs, to garnish

Preheat the oven to 220°c/200°c fan.

Chop the baby potatoes into quarters so they're all similar in size.

Place the potatoes into a large ovenproof dish along with the chicken thighs. Top with the garlic, parsley, thyme and salt.

Mix the ingredients well and place the dish in the preheated oven for 20 minutes.

Meanwhile, blitz the bread and garlic granules in a blender to make the breadcrumb topping.

Stir the parmesan and chopped parsley into the breadcrumbs, then sprinkle this over the chicken and potatoes, making sure all everything is coated.

Cook in the oven for another 15-20 minutes or until the chicken and potatoes are cooked through.

Garnish with some fresh parsley. Serve and enjoy.

Tips: I like to serve this with some tenderstem broccoli, but roasted Mediterranean vegetables on page 172 would be really tasty with the traybake too.

Here's another one pot rice dish: what's not to love about them? They're so quick and easy for those busy weekday dinners and the whole family enjoys them. Chicken and chorizo is a combination that always goes down well at my house.

One Pot Chicken and Chorizo Rice

Servings: 4 | Prep time: 5 minutes | Cooking time: 20 minutes

50g chorizo, sliced

500g chicken breast, diced

1 tbsp smoked paprika

1 tbsp garlic granules

1 tbsp oregano

½ tbsp parsley

1 tsp salt

1 onion, diced

2 peppers, diced

2 cloves of garlic, grated

1 tbsp white wine vinegar

250g basmati rice

600ml chicken stock

80g grated mozzarella

Start by frying the chicken and chorizo with all the seasonings and salt in a large frying pan with a lid.

Once the chorizo oils have been released and the chicken has started to brown, add the diced onion and peppers.

When they have softened, add the garlic and cook for another few minutes.

Now add the white wine vinegar and allow that to cook out for a minute.

Add the uncooked basmati rice and give it a good mix before adding the stock to the pan.

Turn the heat right down low and pop the lid on. Cook for about 10-15 minutes or until all the stock has been absorbed and the rice is fully cooked, adding more liquid if needed.

Fluff the rice with a fork, sprinkle with the grated mozzarella, then serve and enjoy.

Tips: When the rice is cooked, try not to stir it as it will become quite stodgy. Instead, fluff it with a fork so that the grains are separated.

COMFORT MEALS

Tender minced beef in a cheesy sauce with peppers and onions, all topped with crispy, cheesy potatoes? Sounds like heaven to me.

Philly Cheesesteak and Potato Bake

Servings: 4 | Prep time: 10 minutes | Cooking time: 20 minutes

800g potatoes, cubed

1 tbsp garlic granules

1 tbsp smoked paprika

1 tsp salt

Cooking oil spray

500g lean beef mince

Salt and pepper

1 onion, finely diced

3 peppers, finely diced

2 cloves of garlic, finely grated

1 tbsp plain flour

200ml milk, warmed

300ml chicken stock

2 tsp mustard (optional)

60g grated extra mature cheddar

60g grated mozzarella

Preheat the oven to 220°c/200°c fan or an air fryer to 180°c.

In a large bowl, mix the cubed potatoes with the seasonings and some oil spray, then pop them in the oven or air fryer for 15-20 minutes.

Meanwhile, fry the beef in a large pan with some salt and pepper until browned and starting to go crispy.

Add the onion and peppers to the beef and cook until soft. Stir in the garlic and cook for a further minute or so, then add the plain flour.

Mix well and cook off the flour for a minute or so, then begin to add the milk and stock bit by bit, stirring continuously until the sauce has thickened.

Stir the mustard (if using) and cheddar into the beef mixture, then season to taste.

Transfer to an ovenproof dish, place the cooked potatoes on top and then sprinkle with the mozzarella. Pop under a hot grill until golden and bubbling.

Serve and enjoy.

Tips: Once cooked, you can keep this meal in the fridge for up to 3 days to enjoy later. It's also suitable for home freezing and will last for up to 3 months.

This is one of those meals that I could eat over and over again. It's got that familiar taste of Caesar dressing but in a warming hearty dish. I love it served with smashed new potatoes and veggies.

Garlic Chicken in Creamy Caesar Sauce

Servings: 4 | Prep time: 10 minutes | Cooking time: 30 minutes

4 chicken breasts

1 tbsp garlic granules

1 tbsp parsley

1 onion, finely diced

150g lean bacon, diced

3 cloves of garlic, grated

4 tbsp Caesar dressing

300ml hot chicken stock

120ml light single cream

40g parmesan, finely grated

Salt and pepper, to taste

Shop-bought croutons (or you could make your own)

Fresh parsley and parmesan, to garnish (optional)

Preheat the oven to 200°c/180°c fan.

Season the chicken breasts with the garlic and parsley, then fry until starting to brown. Remove from the pan and place in the oven for 25 minutes, or until cooked through.

Meanwhile, fry off the onions and bacon until the onions are soft, then add the garlic.

Cook for another minute and then stir in the Caesar dressing.

Once combined, add the chicken stock and cream, then allow the sauce to reduce for 10 minutes, or until it has thickened.

Once thickened, add the parmesan and mix well. Season with salt and pepper as needed.

Add the cooked chicken back to the pan and top the dish with croutons, parmesan, and parsley to taste. Serve and enjoy.

Tips: You could lower the calories in this dish by using a light Caesar dressing. You could also swap the cream for cream cheese or another alternative.

This dish combines two classic dinners to make one delicious plate of comfort food. Meatballs always go down well with my children, but sometimes it's nice to have a change from pasta, so this makes a great alternative.

Meatball Cottage Pie

Servings: 4 | Prep time: 10 minutes | Cooking time: 40 minutes

800g potatoes, peeled and chopped

20 meatballs (approximately)

1 onion, finely diced

3 cloves of garlic, finely grated

1 tbsp tomato purée

1 tbsp white wine vinegar

500ml passata

1 beef stock cube

120ml light single cream

1 tbsp butter

50-100ml milk

120g grated cheddar

Put the potatoes on to boil in a large pan of salted water.

Meanwhile, fry off your meatballs until browned in a large pan.

Once the meatballs have browned, add the onion and cook until soft.

Add the garlic, tomato purée and white wine vinegar to the meatballs and cook for another minute or so.

Now add the passata and stock cube, mixing well. Bring to a simmer, then stir in the cream.

Once the potatoes are cooked through, drain thoroughly and then mash them in the pan, adding the butter and milk until you have the desired consistency.

Place the meatballs and sauce into an ovenproof dish and top with the mash.

Sprinkle over the cheese and place into the oven for 20 minutes or until the cheese has melted. Serve and enjoy.

Tips: If you want to make this dinner speedier you can always just pop it under the grill to melt the cheese. Just make sure the meatballs are fully cooked before you do.

If you love fajitas, then you're going to love this dish! There are so many ways to serve it too; we love it with new potatoes and crusty bread, but it would also work well with rice, pasta or even mashed potatoes to soak up all that sauce.

Mexican Chicken in Creamy Fajita Sauce

Servings: 4 | Prep time: 5 minutes | Cooking time: 20 minutes

4 chicken breasts

3-4 tbsp fajita seasoning, to taste

1 tsp salt, or to taste

50g chorizo, sliced

2 red onions, finely sliced

3 peppers, finely sliced

3 cloves of garlic, finely grated

1 tbsp tomato purée

1 tbsp white wine vinegar

400ml hot chicken stock

120ml light single cream

Handful of fresh coriander (optional)

Preheat the oven to 200°c/180°c fan or an air fryer to 180°c.

Start by covering the chicken breasts in half the fajita seasoning. Fry them off until they're sealed on both sides and golden brown.

Put them in the oven or air fryer for around 20-30 minutes or until fully cooked.

Meanwhile, use the same frying pan to cook the chorizo. Once the oils start coming out, add the onions and peppers and cook until they're starting to soften.

Stir in the garlic and the remaining fajita seasoning, cook for a few minutes, then add the tomato purée and white wine vinegar.

Allow that to cook out before adding the chicken stock and cream.

Once the stock and cream have reduced to make a thicker sauce, add the cooked chicken breasts back into the pan and sprinkle over the coriander. Serve and enjoy.

Tips: If you don't want this to be too spicy, you can always swap half the fajita seasoning for smoked paprika and garlic granules, or you can buy very mild fajita seasonings. If you do like spice, feel free to add some chilli flakes to give the sauce more of a kick.

This coconut and chicken combination is a simple but very delicious curry. It's one of my favourites to make on a Friday night to keep away the takeaway cravings.

Coconut, Chicken, and Potato Curry

Servings: 4 | Prep time: 10 minutes | Cooking time: 20 minutes

1 tbsp oil

1 onion, finely diced

2 tsp garlic purée

2 tsp ginger purée

1 tsp ground cumin

1 tsp ground turmeric

2 tsp ground coriander

1 tsp garam masala

1 tsp salt

500g chicken breast, diced

500g potatoes, cubed

300ml chicken stock

400ml light coconut milk

Fresh chilli and coriander, to garnish

Start by adding the oil to a frying pan over a medium-low heat. Add the diced onion and fry until soft.

Once the onions are fried, stir in the garlic and ginger purée and cook for another minute or so.

Then add the cumin, turmeric, coriander, garam masala, and salt, mixing well so that the spices are evenly distributed.

Cook this for a few minutes, being careful not to burn the spices.

Add the chicken and potatoes to the pan and fry them off until the chicken has browned.

Pour in the chicken stock and cook for a further 10 minutes or until the potatoes have softened, then add the coconut milk and stir well.

Turn the heat right down and cook for another 4-5 minutes or until the chicken and potatoes are cooked through.

Serve and enjoy garnished with sliced chilli and chopped coriander if you like.

Tips: We love to serve this with some rotis, which is a tasty Indian style flatbread. You can also serve with rice on the side and maybe a naan too if you're feeling extra hungry.

Creamy, cheesy, and spicy is such an incredible combination and this dish has it all! When I first made this dish, I wasn't 100% sure if the kids would enjoy it but it's fast become a family favourite.

Creamy Piri-Piri Chicken and Potato Bake

Servings: 4 | Prep time: 10 minutes | Cooking time: 20 minutes

500g chicken, diced

1 onion, finely sliced

3 peppers, finely sliced

2-3 tbsp piri-piri seasoning, to taste

2 cloves of garlic, finely grated

1 tbsp tomato purée

4 tbsp Nando's Peri-Peri Sauce (I use the lemon and herb flavour)

300ml chicken stock

120ml light single cream

120g grated cheese (I use a mix of cheddar, Red Leicester, and mozzarella)

Fresh parsley, chilli jam and Nando's Perinaise, to garnish (optional)

For the potatoes

500g potatoes, cubed

1 tbsp piri-piri seasoning

1 tbsp garlic granules

1 tsp salt

Preheat the oven to 220°c/200°c fan or an air fryer to 180°c.

Mix the cubed potatoes with the seasonings and pop them in the air fryer or oven for 15-20 minutes.

Meanwhile, cook the chicken, onion, and peppers along with the seasoning in a large ovenproof pan. Once cooked, add the garlic, tomato purée and peri-peri sauce to the chicken and cook for a minute or so.

Pour the stock and cream into the pan and cook until they have formed a thick sauce, then add the cooked potatoes.

Give it a good mix, top with the grated cheese and pop under the grill until golden and bubbling.

Garnish with a sprinkle of chopped parsley, dollops of chilli jam and a drizzle of Nando's Perinaise if using, then serve and enjoy.

This recipe has all the flavours of fajitas but in a layered lasagne covered in a delicious béchamel. This really is comfort food at its very best.

Fajita Lasagne

Servings: 4 | Prep time: 5 minutes | Cooking time: 30-40 minutes

1 onion, finely diced

2 peppers, finely diced

2 cloves of garlic, finely grated

50g chorizo, sliced

500g lean chicken mince

2 tbsp fajita seasoning

1 tbsp tomato purée

500g passata

1 chicken stock cube

8 lasagne sheets

For the béchamel sauce

2 tbsp light butter

2 tbsp plain flour

300ml milk, warmed

1 tsp mustard (optional)

120g cheddar, finely grated

Salt and pepper, to taste

Fresh coriander or parsley, to garnish

In a large frying pan, fry off the onion and peppers until soft and then add the garlic and chorizo.

Mix well and allow to cook for a few minutes and then add the chicken mince and seasoning.

Cook until it starts to brown and then add the tomato purée. Mix well to combine the ingredients.

Once mixed, add the passata and the chicken stock and stir well. Allow to cook for 20 minutes. Preheat the oven to 200°c/180°c fan.

Meanwhile, make your béchamel. Melt the butter in a pan, add the flour and mix, forming a roux. Allow it to cook out for a few minutes.

Add the warmed milk slowly, bit by bit, stirring continuously until you get a thick sauce.

Stir in the mustard and half the cheese, then season with salt and pepper to taste. Set the pan aside off the heat.

In an ovenproof dish, layer the mince mixture and the lasagne sheets. Top with the béchamel sauce and then sprinkle the remaining cheese on top. Pop it in the oven for 30-45 minutes or until cooked through.

Garnish with fresh coriander or parsley. Serve and enjoy.

Tips: For some extra flavour, add some chilli flakes into the béchamel for a little extra kick.

Buffalo sauce is one of my new favourite things! I only discovered how much I enjoyed it recently and since then I've been a little obsessed. Paired with the creamy ranch dressing, this really is a dream dish.

Chicken, Bacon, Buffalo, and Ranch Potato Bake

Servings: 4 | Prep time: 10 minutes | Cooking time: 25 minutes

800g potatoes, cubed

1 ½ tbsp garlic granules

1 tbsp smoked paprika

4 tbsp buffalo sauce

2 tsp salt

500g chicken, diced

1 onion, finely sliced

150g bacon, diced

½ tbsp onion granules

1 tsp each dill, parsley and tarragon

2 cloves of garlic, finely grated

4 tbsp ranch dressing

300ml chicken stock

120ml light single cream

120g mozzarella, grated

Preheat the oven to 220°c/200°c fan or an air fryer to 180°c.

Mix the cubed potatoes with 1 tablespoon of the garlic granules, the smoked paprika and buffalo sauce, and 1 teaspoon of the salt. Place them in the oven or air fryer for 15-20 minutes.

Meanwhile in a pan, fry off the chicken, onion, and bacon along with the remaining half tablespoon of garlic granules and teaspoon of salt, the onion granules, dill, parsley, and tarragon. Mix the ingredients well.

Once cooked, add the grated garlic and ranch dressing. Cook for a further minute or so and then add the stock and cream. Stir well.

Cook until a thick sauce has formed and then place in an ovenproof dish. Scatter the cooked potatoes evenly on top.

Sprinkle the mozarella over the potatoes and pop the dish under the grill until golden and bubbling. Serve and enjoy.

Tips: If you're not too keen on the spice of the buffalo sauce, you can reduce the amount added to the potatoes by half.

This lovely light meal is packed full of flavour, but is also really quick and easy to make, taking less than 30 minutes from start to finish.

Thai-Inspired Salmon Curry

Servings: 4 | Prep time: 5 minutes | Cooking time: 20 minutes

1 tbsp oil

1 onion, finely diced

2 tsp garlic purée

2 tsp ginger purée

1 stick of lemongrass

2 kaffir lime leaves

1 red chilli (optional)

2 tsp ground coriander

1 tsp ground cumin

1 tsp ground turmeric

1 tsp salt

200ml chicken or fish stock

400ml light coconut milk

2 skinless salmon fillets, cubed

200g trimmed green beans

Fresh chilli and coriander, to garnish

Start by frying the onion in the oil in a large frying pan on a medium to low heat.

Once soft, add the garlic purée and ginger purée to cook for another minute or so.

Bash the lemongrass with a rolling pin, then add it to the pan with the lime leaves and red chilli, if using. Now add all the ground spices and salt to the pan.

Mix well and cook for a few minutes, being careful not to burn the spices.

Add the stock and coconut milk to the pan, then let it simmer for 5 minutes.

Turn the heat right down before adding the salmon and green beans.

Stir gently and cook for 4-5 minutes or until the fish flakes easily and the beans are cooked through.

Remove the lemongrass and lime leaves. Garnish with the chilli and coriander, then serve and enjoy.

Tips: If you can't get hold of lemongrass or lime leaves, just use a teaspoon of lemongrass paste or purée. This is usually available in most major supermarkets.

This isn't your traditional cottage pie by any means, but if you're looking for a tasty and comforting dinner, then here it is.

Taco Cottage Pie

Servings: 4 | Prep time: 10 minutes | Cooking time: 1 hour

1 onion, finely diced

2 peppers, finely diced

2 cloves of garlic, finely grated

500g 5% fat beef mince

1 tsp each salt and pepper

1 packet of taco seasoning

1 tbsp tomato purée

400ml beef stock

800g potatoes, peeled and chopped

4 tsp beef gravy granules (optional)

1 tbsp light butter

50-100ml milk

60g grated cheese (I use a mix of cheddar, mozzarella, and Red Leicester)

Fresh chilli and coriander, to garnish

Tips: This recipe is great for meal prep too, as you can portion it up and keep it in the fridge for up to 3 days. It can also be frozen.

Cook the diced onion and peppers in a large pan until soft.

Add the garlic and fry for another minute or so, then add the beef mince and seasoning.

Once the beef mince has browned, add the tomato purée and mix well.

Add the beef stock to the pan and allow to cook on low for at least 30 minutes (the longer the better until you have a rich ragu).

Meanwhile, pop your potatoes on to boil in a pan of salted water and preheat the oven to 200°c/180°c fan.

If you want the beef mixture to be a little thicker, stir in the gravy granules until dissolved.

Once boiled, drain the potatoes and mash them with the butter and enough milk to reach your preferred consistency.

Put the beef mixture into an ovenproof dish, then top with the mash and sprinkle over the grated cheese.

Place in the oven for 20 minutes or until piping hot, golden, and bubbling.

Garnish with the chilli and coriander if using, then serve and enjoy.

Flaky white fish in a deliciously fragrant tomato sauce: this dish is low in calories but high in flavour.

Fragrant Fish Curry

Servings: 4 | Prep time: 5 minutes | Cooking time: 20 minutes

1 tbsp oil

1 onion, finely diced

2 tsp garlic purée

2 tsp ginger purée

2 tsp ground coriander

1 tsp ground cumin

1 tsp ground turmeric

1 tsp garam masala

½ tsp chilli powder, or to taste

1 tsp salt

1 tin of chopped tomatoes

200ml chicken or fish stock

4 firm white fish fillets, cubed (I use cod)

Fresh chilli and coriander, to garnish

Start by frying the onion in the oil in a large frying pan on a medium-low heat.

Once soft, add the garlic purée and ginger purée to cook for another minute or so.

Now add all the ground spices and salt to the pan. Mix well and cook for a few minutes, being careful not to burn the spices.

Add the tinned tomatoes and stock, then let it simmer for 5 minutes.

Turn the heat right down before adding the fish. Stir gently and cook for 4-5 minutes or until the fish flakes easily.

Garnish with the chilli and coriander, then serve and enjoy.

Tips: Make sure you taste the curry to check the seasoning before serving, as it may need a little more salt.

Bolognese has always been a family favourite of mine, as it is with most families. Growing up I always had my Bolognese made with pesto, so I thought I'd give this a try. It went down a storm!

Bolognese and Pesto Potato Bake

Servings: 4 | Prep time: 10 minutes | Cooking time: 35 minutes

1 onion, diced

2 medium carrots, diced

2 peppers, sliced or diced

2 cloves of garlic, finely grated

150g smoked bacon, diced

500g 5% fat beef mince

1 tbsp Italian mixed herbs

1 tbsp tomato purée

1 beef stock cube

500g passata

800g potatoes, cubed

1 tbsp each garlic granules, oregano and salt

4 tbsp pesto (red or green)

60g extra mature cheddar, grated

60g mozzarella, grated

Salt and pepper, to taste

Preheat the oven to 220°c/200°c fan or an air fryer to 190°c.

In a frying pan, fry off the onion, carrots, and peppers until soft, then add the grated garlic.

Add the bacon and cook for a few minutes, then add the beef mince and cook until brown.

Add the mixed herbs, tomato purée, stock cube, and passata to the mince mixture. Cook on a low heat for at least 30 minutes, longer if you have time.

Meanwhile, mix the cubed potatoes with the garlic granules, oregano, salt, and pesto to coat well. Place them in the preheated oven or air fryer for 15-20 minutes until cooked through.

Top the Bolognese sauce with the cooked potatoes in an ovenproof dish, then sprinkle with the cheddar and mozzarella.

Place under the grill or in the oven until golden and bubbling.

Serve and enjoy.

This recipe is a great quick and easy midweek meal that can be cooked and on the table in 30 minutes. The combination of honey and mustard is a classic and it goes so well with the pork.

Creamy Honey Mustard Pork

Servings: 4 | Prep time: 5 minutes | Cooking time: 25 minutes

4 pork loin steaks

Salt and pepper

1 onion, finely chopped

2 cloves of garlic, grated

2 tbsp Dijon mustard

1 tbsp honey

300ml chicken or pork stock

120ml light single cream

Fresh parsley, to garnish

Preheat the oven to 220°c/200°c fan or an air fryer to 180°c.

Season the pork steaks, then fry them in a hot frying pan on both sides to seal them.

Take the pork steaks out of the pan and place them in the oven on a baking tray or in the air fryer for 20 minutes or until fully cooked.

Meanwhile, fry off the onion in the same pan. Once softened, stir in the garlic, mustard and honey. Mix well so that the ingredients are combined.

Once combined, add the chicken stock and cream, stir, and cook until reduced to form a thick sauce.

Add the pork back to the pan, and cover with the sauce, topped with some fresh parsley.

Serve and enjoy.

Tips: I like to serve this with mashed potatoes and greens. It would also go really well with rice or new potatoes as a side.

Chicken, chorizo, and pesto is a combination of flavours that I could never get bored of. The pesto on the potatoes works perfectly with the rich tomato sauce, making this recipe a go-to.

Chicken, Chorizo and Pesto Potato Bake

Servings: 4 | Prep time: 10 minutes | Cooking time: 20 minutes

500g potatoes, cubed

2 tbsp garlic granules

2 tbsp smoked paprika

1 tsp salt

4 tbsp reduced-fat pesto (red or green)

500g chicken, diced

1 onion, finely sliced

50g chorizo, sliced

2 cloves of garlic, finely grated

1 tbsp tomato purée

1 tbsp white wine vinegar

500g passata

120ml light single cream

1 chicken stock pot or cube

120g mozzarella, grated

Preheat the oven to 220°c/200°c fan or an air fryer to 180°c.

In a large bowl, mix the cubed potatoes with half the garlic granules, paprika and salt. Add the pesto and mix until combined, then pop them in the preheated oven or air fryer for 15-20 minutes.

Meanwhile, in a large pan cook off the chicken, onion, and chorizo along with the remaining garlic granules and paprika.

Stir in the garlic and tomato purée, mixing well. Add the white wine vinegar and stir again.

Cook for a minute and then add the passata, cream and stock pot, mixing well until all the ingredients are combined.

Cook for another 5 minutes and then add the cooked potatoes from the oven or air fryer.

Place the mixture into an ovenproof dish, top with the cheese and then pop under the grill until golden and bubbling. Serve and enjoy.

Tips: To serve this for dinner, I like to add roasted Mediterranean vegetables on the side for extra flavour. The recipe for this can be found on page 172.

Creamy chicken and bacon is one of my favourite pie fillings. So, why not swap the pastry lid for a tasty mashed potato topping?

Chicken and Bacon Cottage Pie

Servings: 4 | Prep time: 10 minutes | Cooking time: 40 minutes

800g potatoes, peeled and chopped

500g chicken breast, diced

150g bacon, diced

1 onion, finely diced

2 cloves of garlic, finely grated

1 tbsp tarragon

2 tbsp plain flour

200ml milk, warmed

200ml chicken stock

1 tsp mustard (optional)

100ml milk

1 tbsp light butter

60g extra mature cheddar

1 tsp salt and pepper, or to taste

Put your potatoes into a pan of boiling water with plenty of salt.

Preheat the oven to 200°c/180°c fan.

Meanwhile, fry off the chicken breast in a large pan, adding salt and pepper to taste, then add the bacon and fry until crisp.

Add the onion and cook until soft, then stir in the garlic and tarragon.

Cook for another couple of minutes, then add the flour and mix well.

Cook the flour out for a couple of minutes and then slowly add in the milk and stock, bit by bit, making sure to stir continuously.

Once you have a thick sauce, add the mustard if using and mix well. Season the pie filling with salt and pepper to taste.

Drain the cooked potatoes, then mash them with the milk and butter.

Place the chicken mix into an ovenproof dish and top with the mash, then grate the cheddar and sprinkle it on top.

Place your pie in the preheated oven for 20 minutes or until piping hot, with the cheese golden and bubbling. Serve and enjoy.

Tips: Instead of the bacon, an alternative to try is ham or gammon, which also works really well as a replacement.

Lasagne is my little boy's favourite, so it has become a much-loved regular in our house. However, sometimes it's nice to mix it up a bit so I've added a couple of alternative options to tweak the classic béchamel sauce in this recipe.

Lasagne Three Ways

Servings: 4 | Prep time: 10 minutes | Cooking time: 1-2 hours

500g lean beef mince

150g smoked bacon, diced

1 onion, finely diced

2 medium carrots, finely diced

3 peppers, finely diced

2 cloves of garlic, minced

1 tbsp Italian mixed herbs

1 tbsp tomato purée

500g passata

1 beef stock pot

Salt and pepper

8 lasagne sheets

120g grated cheddar

For the béchamel

2 tbsp light butter

2 tbsp plain flour

300ml milk, warmed

1 tsp mustard (optional)

2 tbsp pesto (optional)

100g Boursin (optional)

Start by browning the beef mince and bacon in a large pan.

Once browned, add the onion, carrots, and peppers to the pan. Stir well and cook until softened, then add the garlic and cook for a minute.

Mix in the herbs and tomato purée, cook for a minute and then add the passata and beef stock pot. Season to taste with salt and pepper.

Allow this to cook for at least 20 minutes, but if you have time cook the ragu for an hour on a low heat.

Meanwhile, make your béchamel sauce. Start by melting the butter in a pan.

Add the flour to the melted butter and mix to form a paste (known as a roux). Allow this to cook for a few minutes.

Slowly pour the warmed milk into the pan bit by bit, stirring continuously until you get a thick sauce with no lumps in.

Now add the mustard, pesto or Boursin to the béchamel if using and then season to taste with salt and pepper. Set the sauce aside for now and preheat the oven to 200°c/180°c fan.

Layer the mince and the lasagne sheets in a large ovenproof dish, then top with the béchamel and sprinkle with the grated cheddar.

Pop your lasagne in the preheated oven to cook for 30-45 minutes or until cooked through, golden and bubbling. Serve and enjoy.

The calorie count is 574 with pesto or 629 with Boursin.

SIDES AND SMALL BITES

These little bites of heaven are a perfect side dish at a BBQ and they're even delicious when eaten cold the next day.

Honey BBQ Bacon Potatoes

Servings: 4 | Prep time: 5 minutes | Cooking time: 35 minutes

800g baby potatoes, quartered

1 tbsp smoked paprika

½ tbsp paprika

½ tbsp garlic granules

½ tbsp oregano

½ tbsp parsley

1 tsp salt

2 tbsp BBQ sauce

2 tbsp honey

150g diced smoked bacon

Fresh parsley, to garnish (optional)

Preheat the oven to 220°c/200°c fan or an air fryer to 180°c.

In a large bowl, mix the potatoes with the smoked paprika, paprika, garlic granules, oregano, parsley and salt.

Pop them in the oven or air fryer for 20-30 minutes.

Once cooked, take them out and pour over the BBQ sauce, honey and diced bacon.

Give them a good mix and then put them back in the oven or air fryer for another 10 minutes, until cooked.

Once done, sprinkle over the parsley.

Serve and enjoy.

Tips: If you wanted to make this dish slightly quicker, you can parboil the potatoes first and then pop everything in the oven or air fryer together for 15-20 minutes to crisp up.

These crispy little mouthfuls are spicy, slightly sweet, and very moreish. We love them with salad and fries on the side but they're also great in a wrap or sandwich.

Crispy Cajun Chicken Bites

Servings: 4 | Prep time: 5 minutes | Cooking time: 15 minutes

500g chicken breast, diced

1 ½ tbsp Cajun seasoning

1 ½ tbsp smoked paprika

1 tbsp garlic granules

1 tsp salt

1 egg or egg white, whisked

60g cornflakes, crushed

Cooking oil spray

4 tbsp mayonnaise

1 tbsp honey

½ tbsp lemon or lime juice

1 tsp chilli flakes

Parsley, to garnish

Preheat the oven to 220°c/200°c fan or an air fryer to 180°c.

Season the chicken with 1 tablespoon each of the Cajun seasoning and smoked paprika, plus the garlic granules and salt.

Coat the chicken pieces in the whisked egg and then cover with the crushed cornflakes.

Spray the chicken bites with oil and put them in the air fryer or oven for 10-15 minutes.

Put the mayo, honey and lemon or lime juice into a bowl with the remaining smoked paprika and Cajun seasoning. Mix well to combine.

Once the chicken bites are cooked, pop them into the sauce and coat well.

Sprinkle with the chilli flakes, garnish with sprigs of parsley, then serve and enjoy.

Tips: You could swap the cornflakes for breadcrumbs, crushed crisps, or a different cereal like Rice Krispies.

These quick and easy tikka skewers are perfect for the summer months. Whether on the barbecue, in a salad or even a sandwich, you're bound to keep going back for more.

Chicken Tikka Skewers

Servings: 4 | Prep time: 5 minutes | Cooking time: 10 minutes

500g chicken breast, diced

200g natural fat-free yoghurt

½ lemon, juiced

2 tsp garlic purée

2 tsp ginger purée

2 tsp ground coriander

1 tsp ground cumin

1 tsp ground turmeric

1 tsp garam masala

1 tsp paprika

1 tsp salt

½ tsp ground cinnamon

½ tsp chilli powder (optional)

Mix all the ingredients together in a large bowl and leave to marinate for 30 minutes. If you have time, leave overnight.

Preheat the oven to 220°c/200°c fan or an air fryer to 180°c.

Thread the marinated chicken onto your skewers.

Cook for around 10-15 minutes in the oven or air fryer until cooked through.

Serve and enjoy.

Tips: If you are using wooden skewers, make sure to soak them in water first to prevent them from burning. For me, metal skewers work best as they help to cook the chicken from the inside.

I think the title of this recipe says it all! What's not to love about sticky sweet hoisin sauce, and when you pair that with crispy fries… heaven in a bowl.

Sticky Hoisin Fries

Servings: 4 | Prep time: 10 minutes | Cooking time: 25 minutes

800g potatoes, chipped

2 cloves of garlic, finely grated

5cm cube of ginger, finely grated

3 tbsp hoisin sauce

2 tbsp honey

1 tbsp soy sauce

1 tsp Chinese five spice

To garnish (optional)

Sliced red chilli, to taste

4 spring onions, sliced

1-2 tsp sesame seeds

Preheat the oven to 220°c/200°c fan or an air fryer to 180°c.

Put the chipped potatoes into the air fryer or oven to cook for 20-25 minutes.

Meanwhile, mix all the other ingredients together, except the garnish, in a large pan and cook until sticky.

Add the cooked fries to the pan and coat with the sticky sauce.

Garnish with the chilli, spring onion and sesame seeds.

Serve and enjoy.

Tips: You can swap the potatoes for ready-made fries to make this dish even quicker and easier.

I don't know about you but I absolutely love a wrap or a sandwich for dinner and this one is no exception. You can serve this with some wedges and salad on the side to bulk it out a little more too.

Cheesy Cajun Sausage Wrap

Servings: 4 | Prep time: 5 minutes | Cooking time: 10 minutes

8 sausages

2 peppers, diced

1 tbsp smoked paprika

1-2 tbsp Cajun seasoning

Salt and pepper, to taste

120g grated cheese (I use a mix of mozzarella, cheddar, and Red Leicester)

½ red onion, finely diced

4 tbsp lighter mayonnaise

Fresh coriander (optional)

4 wraps

Peel the sausages, discarding the skins, and break them up into bite-size pieces.

Fry the sausage and red pepper with the smoked paprika and Cajun seasoning, seasoning to taste with salt and pepper.

Put the sausage mixture into a bowl with the cheese, red onion, mayo, and coriander if using. Mix to combine.

Pop it all in a wrap, fold and toast in a dry pan or air fry at 180°c for 5 minutes to seal it shut.

Serve and enjoy.

Tips: Prep the sausages and peppers first, then get everything else ready while the sausages and peppers are cooking to save time.

These bites are so versatile! They're incredible in a wrap or sandwich but also just as delicious served with some potato wedges and salad. The combination of sweet and spicy makes them so moreish, you'll be wanting to eat the lot.

Crispy Bang Bang Chicken Bites

Servings: 4 | Prep time: 4 minutes | Cooking time: 15 minutes

500g chicken breast, diced

1 ½ tbsp smoked paprika

1 ½ tbsp garlic granules

1 ½ tbsp oregano

1 tsp salt

60g cornflakes, crushed

1 egg or egg white, whisked

2 tbsp sweet chilli sauce

2 tbsp mayonnaise

1 tbsp honey

1 tsp paprika

1 tsp chilli flakes (or to taste)

Spring onion, to garnish

Preheat the oven to 220°c/200°c fan or an air fryer to 180°c.

Season the chicken with 1 tablespoon each of the smoked paprika, garlic granules, and oregano, plus the salt.

Season the crushed cornflakes with the remaining smoked paprika, garlic, and oregano in a shallow bowl. Coat the chicken in the whisked egg and then cover with the seasoned cornflakes.

Pop the coated chicken in the oven or air fryer for 10-15 minutes, depending on how big the pieces are, until cooked through.

Meanwhile, combine the sweet chilli sauce, mayo, honey, paprika, and chilli flakes in a bowl. Add the hot chicken bites to this sauce and turn to coat them well.

Garnish with sliced spring onion, then serve and enjoy.

Tips: If you like a bit of spice, you can always add more chilli flakes or even some hot sauce to the sweet chilli and mayo mixture. You can also add less if you're not a big fan of spice; it will still be delicious!

In this recipe, the sticky hoisin sauce alongside the rich beef and crunchy freshness of cucumber and spring onion is a marriage made in heaven. This dish reminds me of classic Chinese takeaway pancakes but with more substance.

Hoisin Beef Burrito

Servings: 4 | Prep time: 5 minutes | Cooking time: 15 minutes

1 tbsp oil

500g lean beef mince

½ tbsp Chinese five spice

1 tbsp garlic granules

2 peppers, finely diced

3 cloves of garlic, finely grated

5cm cube of ginger, finely grated

1 tsp chilli flakes, or to taste

3 spring onions, thinly sliced

4 wraps

250g cooked rice

½ cucumber, thinly sliced

For the sauce

1 tbsp each dark & light soy sauce

4 tbsp hoisin sauce

1 tbsp honey

Heat the oil in a large frying pan until very hot and then add the beef mince. Add the five spice and garlic granules. Mix well.

Once the beef has browned, add the peppers, garlic, ginger, chilli, and 2 of the spring onions.

Cook for a few minutes, being careful not to burn the garlic, then add the dark and light soy sauce, hoisin sauce and honey to make a sauce.

Once sticky and crispy, take out of the pan and serve in a bowl.

Assemble the wraps with the cooked rice, cucumber, remaining spring onions, and the hoisin beef.

Serve and enjoy.

Tips: You can cook the rice yourself using a rice cooker, however for ease I bought the microwave packets of ready-made rice.

There is no better summer side dish than roasted Mediterranean vegetables. It screams sunshine and is perfect for those warm nights when you don't want to stand over the hob.

Roasted Mediterranean Vegetables

Servings: 4 | Prep time: 5 minutes | Cooking time: 20 minutes

3 peppers, sliced

2 red onions, sliced

1 courgette, sliced

250g cherry tomatoes

6 cloves of garlic

1 tbsp oil

1 tbsp garlic granules

1 tsp oregano

1 tsp thyme

1 tsp salt

80g feta, cubed (optional)

Balsamic glaze (optional)

Preheat the oven to 220°c/200°c fan or an air fryer to 180°c.

In a large roasting tin, mix all the ingredients together except the feta and balsamic glaze.

Roast for 20 minutes or until the vegetables are soft and beginning to caramelise.

Crumble over the feta and drizzle with the balsamic glaze.

Serve and enjoy.

Tips: You can remove any of the veggies that you don't want, or add any extras that you'd like, such as new potatoes.

CALORIES 212 PER PORTION

These fries are bursting with aromatic flavours and spices. They make the perfect side for a Friday night 'fakeaway' to share with family or friends.

Masala Fries

Servings: 4 | Prep time: 5 minutes | Cooking time: 25 minutes

800g potatoes

Cooking oil spray

1 tbsp oil

1 onion, finely diced

2 tsp ginger purée

2 tsp garlic purée

2 tsp ground coriander

1 tsp ground cumin

1 tsp ground turmeric

1 tsp garam masala

½ tsp chilli powder

1 tsp salt

1 medium tomato, diced

Fresh chilli and coriander, to garnish

Preheat the oven to 220°c/200°c fan or an air fryer to 180°c.

Peel the potatoes and cut them into fries, spray with oil and cook in the oven or air fryer for about 20-25 minutes.

Meanwhile, heat the oil in a frying pan and fry the onion on a medium heat.

Once the onion is soft, add the ginger and garlic and cook for another few minutes.

Stir in all the spices and salt. Cook for a few minutes, making sure they don't burn.

Add the diced tomato and a splash of water to the pan, then cook until the mixture forms a thick sauce.

When the fries are cooked, put them into the sauce and combine the two together.

Garnish with fresh chilli and coriander, then serve hot and enjoy.

Tips: These masala fries work perfectly with a minted yoghurt dip. Just mix natural yoghurt, mint sauce and a squeeze of lemon juice together, add a pinch of salt to taste, and enjoy!

This easy chicken shawarma recipe is one of those meals that stops takeaway cravings in their tracks. It's so easy to prepare and tastes incredible!

Easy Chicken Shawarma Wrap

Servings: 4 | Prep time: 5 minutes | Cooking time: 30 minutes

500g skinless and boneless chicken thighs

1 large red onion, sliced

2 peppers, sliced

2 tsp garlic purée

2 tsp ginger purée

1 tsp ground cumin

1 tsp ground turmeric

1 tsp ground coriander

1 tsp paprika

½ tsp ground cinnamon

1 tsp chilli flakes (optional)

1 tsp salt

4 wraps

Salad of your choice

For the garlic sauce

4 tbsp mayonnaise

4 tbsp fat-free natural yoghurt

½ lemon, juiced

2 cloves of garlic, grated

Pinch of salt, to taste

Preheat the oven to 220°c/200°c fan or an air fryer to 180°c.

Put the chicken thighs, onion, peppers, garlic purée and ginger purée into a roasting tin. Add the ground cumin, turmeric, coriander, paprika, cinnamon, chilli flakes, and salt. Mix well, ensuring the chicken and vegetables are covered in the spices.

Cook for about 25-30 minutes in the oven or air fryer or until the chicken thighs are cooked through.

For the garlic sauce, simply mix the mayonnaise, yoghurt, lemon juice and garlic in a small bowl. Season with salt to taste.

Once cooked, remove the chicken from the oven and slice the chicken thighs into pieces a similar size to the onion and peppers.

Assemble the wraps with the chicken and vegetables, salad and garlic sauce, then serve and enjoy.

This recipe is one of my favourite ways to cook potatoes! It's easy to do but has maximum flavour. Although they may take a while to cook, I promise you they are worth it! The combination of fresh zingy lemon with garlic and oregano is one that I will never get bored of and can eat again and again.

Greek Lemon and Garlic Potatoes

Servings: 4 | Prep time: 5 minutes | Cooking time: 45-60 minutes

800g potatoes, peeled

1 tbsp olive oil

1 tbsp oregano

1 tsp salt

500ml chicken stock

1 lemon, juiced

6 cloves of garlic, finely grated

Preheat the oven to 220°c/200°c fan or an air fryer to 180°c.

Cut the potatoes into wedges and add to a large roasting tin. Cover the potatoes with the oil and sprinkle over the oregano and salt.

Mix the stock, lemon juice and garlic together, and pour into the roasting tin.

Cook for 45 minutes or until all the stock has been absorbed and the potatoes are crisp and golden.

Give the potatoes a mix halfway through to make sure they're cooking evenly.

Serve and enjoy.

Tips: I find that baking potatoes or Maris Pipers work really well for this dish. They work so well as a side for most meals, but I often have them with gyros or a roast dinner.

I'm not sure this recipe really needs much of an introduction, as it really does speak for itself. Garlic butter heaven in the form of fries.

Garlic Butter Fries

Servings: 4 | Prep time: 5 minutes | Cooking time: 25 minutes

800g potatoes, peeled

Cooking oil spray

4 tbsp light butter

3 tsp garlic purée

1 tbsp finely chopped fresh parsley

½ tsp salt

Preheat the oven to 220°c/200°c fan or an air fryer to 180°c.

Chop your potatoes into fries and spray with oil. Cook in the oven or air fryer for 20-25 minutes.

Meanwhile in a bowl, mix the butter, garlic purée, parsley, and salt.

When the fries are nearly cooked, melt the garlic butter in a large frying pan.

Add the cooked fries into the butter and mix well so that the fries are evenly covered in the garlic butter.

Serve and enjoy.

Tips: These tasty garlic fries are amazing as a side dish for my bacon and cheese smash burger on page 38.

Fajitas are a staple in most homes, mine being one of them. This recipe is all done in the oven or air fryer so it's even easier, especially in the summer when you don't want to be standing over the hob.

Easy Chicken Fajita Wrap

Servings: 4 | Prep time: 5 minutes | Cooking time: 35 minutes

500g skinless and boneless chicken thighs

1 large red onion, sliced

3 peppers, sliced

2 tsp garlic purée

2 tbsp fajita seasoning

4 wraps

Sour cream, guacamole, and salsa to serve (optional)

Preheat the oven to 220°c/200°c fan or an air fryer to 180°c.

Put the chicken thighs, onion, peppers, and garlic purée into a roasting tin. Top with the fajita seasoning and mix well so everything is coated.

Cook in the preheated oven for about 30-35 minutes, until the chicken thighs are cooked through.

Once cooked, slice the chicken thighs up and then assemble the wraps.

Serve alongside sour cream, guacamole and salsa and enjoy.

Tips: I choose to use a mild fajita mix so that my children will enjoy them. However, if you prefer your fajitas with a bit of a kick you could always add some chilli flakes to the wraps for a spicier taste.

This is always my go-to when ordering tapas. There's something about those crispy potatoes, the smoky tomato sauce and zingy garlic aioli that makes me crave them again and again.

Patatas Bravas

Servings: 4 | Prep time: 5 minutes | Cooking time: 20 minutes

800g baby potatoes, quartered

Salt and pepper

1 tbsp oil or cooking oil spray

1 onion, finely diced

2 cloves of garlic, finely diced

1 tbsp tomato purée

1 tbsp smoked paprika

1 tbsp garlic granules

1 tsp chilli flakes

1 tin of chopped tomatoes

Pinch of sugar or sweetener

Fresh parsley, to garnish

For the aioli

1 large clove of garlic, finely grated

4 tbsp light mayonnaise

2 tsp water

Pinch of salt

Preheat the oven to 220°c/200°c fan or an air fryer to 180°c.

Season the potatoes and coat lightly with the oil. Place them in the oven or air fryer for about 20-30 minutes until cooked through and crisp on the outside.

Meanwhile, fry the onion in a pan until soft. Add the garlic and cook for another minute or so, then add the tomato purée and seasonings.

Give the contents of the pan a good mix and then add the chopped tomatoes. Season with the sugar or sweetener and salt to taste. Reduce until it forms a thick sauce.

For the aioli, stir the garlic into the mayonnaise and add a pinch of salt. Stir in the water until it comes together in a pourable consistency.

Assemble the patatas bravas with crispy potatoes in a dish, covered by the tomato sauce and drizzled with aioli. Garnish with fresh parsley, serve and enjoy.

Tips: You can add more or less chilli depending on your personal tastes. I tend to add less for the children and then sprinkle extra chilli flakes over our portions at the end.

Honey roasted vegetables are a classic side for most roast dinners. The natural sweetness of the veggies is enhanced by a drizzle of runny honey which forms a deliciously sticky glaze in the oven.

Honey Roasted Vegetables

Servings: 4 | Prep time: 10 minutes | Cooking time: 40 minutes

2 sweet potatoes

4 medium carrots

2 medium parsnips

1 large red onion

1 bulb of garlic

2 tbsp oil

2 tsp thyme

2 tbsp honey

Salt and pepper

Preheat the oven to 220°c/200°c fan or an air fryer to 180°c. Cut the sweet potatoes, carrots, parsnips and red onion into wedges. Break the garlic bulb into cloves, leaving the skins on.

In an ovenproof dish, mix all the ingredients together apart from the honey. Season with the salt and pepper to taste.

Roast the vegetables for 30 minutes in the oven or air fryer or until they have softened, shaking the dish halfway through.

Take the vegetables out of the oven or air fryer and drizzle over the honey.

Roast the vegetables for 10 minutes, keeping an eye on them to make sure they don't burn.

Remove and squeeze the roasted garlic out of the skins into the dish. Mix until the honey roasted vegetables are coated in the sweet garlic, then serve and enjoy.

Tips: These honey roasted vegetables also make a great side dish for the creamy honey mustard pork on page 148.

This is one of our favourite side dishes to make when we have a barbecue. It always goes down a storm and it's so simple to make with just a few ingredients.

Curried Potato Salad

Servings: 4 | Prep time: 5 minutes | Cooking time: 15 minutes

750g new potatoes, quartered

4 tbsp fat-free natural yoghurt

4 tbsp light mayonnaise

1 tbsp garam masala

1 tbsp mango chutney

Handful of spring onions, finely sliced

Fresh chives and chilli flakes, to garnish (optional)

Put your potatoes on to boil in a pan of salted water for 15 minutes.

Meanwhile, mix the rest of the ingredients together in a bowl and season to taste with salt and pepper.

When the potatoes are cooked through, drain them well, then add to the dressing in the bowl.

Give it a good mix and then garnish with fresh chives and chilli flakes.

Serve and enjoy.

Tips: For a bit of extra flavour, put some fresh mint in the water while boiling your new potatoes.

Conversion Charts

WEIGHTS

25g – 1 oz
50g – 2 oz
100g – 3½ oz
150g – 5 oz
200g – 7 oz
250g – 9 oz
275g – 10 oz
500g – 1 lb 2 oz

LIQUIDS

5ml – 1 tsp
15ml – 1 tbsp
30ml – ⅛ cup
60ml – ¼ cup
75ml – ⅓ cup
125ml – ½ cup
150ml – ⅔ cup
175ml – ¾ cup
250ml – 1 cup

OVEN TEMPERATURES
(CELSIUS TO FAHRENHEIT)

140°c – 275°F
150°c – 300°F
170°c – 325°F
180°c – 350°F
190°c – 375°F
200°c – 400°F
220°c – 425°F

OTHER APPROXIMATE MEASURES

Grated Cheese: 1 cup = 100g
Uncooked Pasta: 1 cup = 100g
Uncooked Rice: 1 cup = 200g

First edition printed in 2023 in the UK
ISBN: 978-1-915538-05-5

Written by: Hollie Wood
Edited by: Katie Fisher & Emily Retford
Photography by: Paul Gregory
Designed by: Paul Cocker, Kate McCann,
& Rhianna Emberson
Sales & PR: Emma Toogood & Lizzy Capps
Contributors: Lis Ellis & Phil Turner
Printed in UK by Bell and Bain Ltd, Glasgow

me:ze
PUBLISHING

Published by Meze Publishing Limited
Unit 1b, 2 Kelham Square
Kelham Riverside
Sheffield S3 8SD
Web: www.mezepublishing.co.uk
Telephone: 0114 275 7709
Email: info@mezepublishing.co.uk